# DATE DUE

|  |  |  |  |
|---|---|---|---|
| ~~JUL 3 '98~~ |  |  |  |
| FE ~~1 0 '98~~ |  |  |  |
|  |  |  |  |
|  |  |  |  |
|  |  |  |  |
|  |  |  |  |
|  |  |  |  |
|  |  |  |  |
|  |  |  |  |
|  |  |  |  |
|  |  |  |  |
|  |  |  |  |
|  |  |  |  |
|  |  |  |  |
|  |  |  |  |
|  |  |  |  |
|  |  |  |  |

The Samuel & Althea Stroum Lectures

IN JEWISH STUDIES

# Gender and Assimilation in Modern Jewish History

## The Roles and Representation of Women

Paula E. Hyman

University of Washington Press
*Seattle & London*

publication may be
rm or by any means,
photocopy, recording,
val system, without
the publisher.

Publication Data

Hyman, Paula, 1946–
Gender and assimilation in modern Jewish history :
the roles and representation of women / Paula E. Hyman.
p.  cm. — (The Samuel & Althea Stroum lectures in Jewish studies)
Includes bibliographical references and index.
ISBN 0-295-97425-7 (cloth). — ISBN 0-295-97426-5 (pbk.)
1. Jews—Cultural assimilation—Europe.   2. Jews—Cultural
assimilation—United States.   3. Jewish women—Europe—Social
conditions.   4. Jewish women—United States—Social conditions.
5. Europe—Ethnic relations.   6. United States—Ethnic relations.
I. Title.   II. Series: Samuel and Althea Stroum lectures
in Jewish studies.
DS148.H93   1995
305.48′696—dc20        94-37932        CIP

# The Samuel & Althea Stroum Lectures
## IN JEWISH STUDIES

Samuel Stroum, businessman, community leader, and philanthropist, by a major gift to the Jewish Federation of Greater Seattle, established the Samuel and Althea Stroum Philanthropic Fund.

In recognition of Mr. and Mrs. Stroum's deep interest in Jewish history and culture, the Board of Directors of the Jewish Federation of Greater Seattle, in cooperation with the Jewish Studies Program of the Henry M. Jackson School of International Studies at the University of Washington, established an annual lectureship at the University of Washington known as the Samuel and Althea Stroum Lectureship in Jewish Studies. This lectureship makes it possible to bring to the area outstanding scholars and interpreters of Jewish thought, thus promoting a deeper understanding of Jewish history, religion, and culture. Such understanding can lead to an enhanced appreciation of the Jewish contributions to the historical and cultural traditions that have shaped the American nation.

The terms of the gift also provide for the publication from time to time of the lectures or other appropriate materials resulting from or related to the lectures.

To my daughters,
JUDITH and ADINA

# Contents

# Preface

I have been interested in the history of Jewish women since my days as a graduate student some twenty years ago. Although my own professional training was conspicuously silent on the subject of women, and gender was a concept of interest only to anthropologists studying primitive tribes, my involvement with feminism at the university and in the Jewish community sparked my curiosity about women in the past and the role of gender in human experience. Beginning with a collaborative effort on the history of Jewish women in America, whenever time permitted I returned to the subject of women in modern Jewish history. As I read more broadly in the growing and ever more sophisticated literature in general women's history and pursued my own research, I became convinced that there was much to say about the relation between gender and the encounter of Jews with the various conditions of modernity. The invitation to offer the Stroum Lectures at the University of Washington in 1992 permitted me to reflect upon the roles and representation of Jewish women as Jews struggled to define a place for themselves in Europe and America. The questions that I raise in this slim volume, though limited to Ashkenazi Jews, will, I hope, stimulate others to investigate the experience of women and gender representations in Sephardi communities and in other parts of the Jewish world, including the prestate *yishuv* and Israeli society.

The publication of this book provides me with the happy opportunity of thanking a series of individuals who contributed to its appearance. Samuel and Althea Stroum's generosity and commitment to Jewish learning provided the framework for the lectures which form the basis of this book. I am most grateful to Professor Hillel Kieval and his colleagues in the University of Washington's Jewish Studies Program for inviting me to Seattle. Their gracious hospitality, ably coordinated by the program's assistant, Dorothy Becker, combined with unusually warm and sunny weather to offer a serene setting for reflecting on my subject in addition to delivering the lectures themselves. The questions from faculty and other members of the audience initiated a process of extending and clarifying my ideas.

At Yale my work in progress on gender and assimilation was assisted by colleagues in a number of settings. I am particularly grateful to the Whitney Humanities Center Fellows and to the Women's Studies Faculty Council, who listened to early versions of my arguments and offered suggestions for further research and refinement of my major points. Two groups of students in my undergraduate course on women and Judaism stimulated my thinking, as did my then graduate student Beth Wenger. It is a pleasure for a scholar to be part of an institution that encourages the building of bridges across fields and disciplines and thereby promotes intellectual creativity.

I was fortunate to work in libraries and archives with rich resources for the study of modern Jewish history. To the staffs of the Jewish National and University Library in Jerusalem, the YIVO Institute, the library of the Jewish Theological Seminary, and the Jewish Division of the New York Public Library, as well as the libraries of Yale, I express my gratitude.

Several colleagues read one or more drafts of this book and offered encouragement, editorial advice, and constructive criticism. At each stage—conducting my research, preparing the lectures for presentation, and transforming the lectures into a book—I could count on Richard Cohen, Debórah Dwork, Marion Kaplan, and Deborah Dash Moore. For fifteen years Marion Kaplan has stimulated my thinking about Jewish women, and her research has been invaluable for my own. As usual, Deborah Moore has spurred me to my best work through her multiple roles as friend, editor, and partner in debate. The book is the better for their concern; I alone am responsible for its deficiencies. Many thanks to my editors Naomi Pascal and Pamela Bruton for their support and commitment to high editorial standards.

My family has shared in this endeavor, listening with more patience than could be expected to tales culled from memoirs of forgotten women. My husband, Stanley Rosenbaum, read each draft with an eye to crafting a narrative for the intelligent but nonspecialist reader. My daughters, Judith and Adina, have inspired me with their continued enthusiasm for this project, even as over the course of two years they heard more about one female activist, Puah Rakowski, than they ever dreamed of. Their lives are the continuation of the tale I have tried to tell, and it is to them that I dedicate this book with great love.

# Gender and Assimilation in Modern Jewish History

## The Roles and Representation of Women

# Introduction

The beginning of my graduate studies in Jewish history co-incided with my introduction to feminism as a social and intellectual movement. That encounter shaped my self-definition as a Jewish woman and opened my eyes to the absence of women from all that I was studying. As a graduate student I became an activist in the nascent Jewish women's movement and joined with two friends in writing a popular history of American Jewish women, *The Jewish Woman in America*, published in 1976.[1] That book, however, was not directly connected to my academic program, and I viewed it as a digression from my "serious work." As a scholar I focused on my chosen area of specialization, the history of modern French Jewry. The field of general women's history was just achieving recognition. Within Judaic studies the first stirrings of interest in recovering the history of Jewish women manifested themselves in the early 1980s and had little impact in the field beyond a small coterie of primarily female scholars and students.

When given the option to prepare papers for academic conferences, however, I increasingly chose subjects related to women's history. The publication of these papers, in particular my anthologized article on the 1902 female-led New York kosher meat boycott, brought the specific experience of Jewish women to the attention of scholars of general women's his-

1. Charlotte Baum, Paula Hyman, and Sonya Michel, *The Jewish Woman in America* (New York: Dial Press, 1976).

3

tory and raised questions about the implications of women's history for Jewish historians.[2] As feminist theory has exploded and historical studies of women have proliferated, I have become all the more eager to apply the exciting perspectives that have emerged in general women's history to the field of Jewish history. The invitation to deliver the 1992 Stroum Lectures offered me an unparalleled opportunity to do so.

Like many historians of modern Jewry, I had addressed the issue of assimilation in many different contexts—examining the adaptation of immigrants from eastern Europe in both French and American settings and exploring the impact of emancipation upon a particular community of traditional Jews, the village Jews of nineteenth-century Alsace. My work on village Jews reflected my desire to prod Jewish historical scholarship to be more inclusive in its concerns, to recognize that the concentration on urban male elites, and on intellectuals in particular, provided only a partial picture of the historical experience of Jews in the modern period. Although the male Jewish leadership of urban Jewish centers determined the agenda of Jewish communities and spoke for all Jews in official documents and in the Jewish press, the experience of most Jews—women and Jewish men who did not reach leadership ranks—was not necessarily subsumed in

2. Paula E. Hyman, "Immigrant Women and Consumer Protest: The New York Kosher Meat Boycott of 1902," *American Jewish History* 70, no. 1 (Sept. 1980): 91–105; reprinted in *The American Jewish Experience*, ed. Jonathan Sarna (New York: Holmes & Meier, 1986), pp. 135–46, and in *Ethnicity and Gender: The Immigrant Woman*, ed. George E. Pozzetta (New York: Garland Publishing, 1991), pp. 81–95. See also my "Culture and Gender: Women in the Immigrant Jewish Community," in *The Legacy of Jewish Migration: 1881 and Its Impact*, ed. David Berger, Social Science Monographs (New York: Brooklyn College Press, 1983), pp. 157–68.

statements by those who represented them in public records. Given the impact of assimilation in modern Jewish history, it seemed critical that interpretations of the ways in which modern Jews adapted to the societies in which they lived and fundamentally reshaped their identities be based upon as wide a segment of the Jewish population as possible. Generalizations about assimilation were useful only insofar as they took into account the specific social contexts in which individual choices became collective behavior. At any time and place, the social contexts of women and men differed because of the gendered nature of social roles.

I have attempted to accomplish two linked tasks in this book: to reclaim the experience of Jewish women as they accommodated to the socioeconomic and ideological challenges of modernity in western and central Europe, eastern Europe, and the United States, particularly in the latter part of the nineteenth century and the beginning of the twentieth; and to explore the role of ideas about gender in the construction of Jewish identity in the modern period. I hope that my research and analysis will stimulate scholars in several disciplines to conduct further studies. My aim is to challenge, and I welcome responses that critically examine my assertions. Most importantly, I hope that scholars in the field of modern Jewish studies who have not specialized in issues of women's history or gender will recognize the potential of research in these areas for expanding and, at times, transforming our understanding of fundamental aspects of Jewish historical and cultural development. Although the inclusion of women and gender in the writing of history is important in itself, it is not, in historian Gerda Lerner's terms, simply a matter of "add women and stir." Feminist scholarship has aspired to, and achieved, more than "filling in the gaps" of information about half of humanity. In historical scholarship it has challenged such basic paradigms of the field as periodization and the determination of what is deemed historically significant. As I have suggested elsewhere,[3] in Jewish historiography of the modern period research on women and gender has already expanded our conceptualization of Jewish religious life to include the subjects of domestic religion and personal spirituality. Women's history has also altered our understanding of the nature and definition of community among Jews and has revealed hitherto unrecognized complexities in the issue of assimilation. With this book, which draws upon studies by many of my colleagues as well as upon my own new research, I hope to demonstrate that to be valid an examination of the processes of Jewish assimilation in the modern and contemporary periods must include women and gender in its design.

In exploring the interaction of gender and assimilation in modern Jewish history, I am well aware that I could not possibly include all aspects of such a complex phenomenon within the format of a series of lectures. All Jews in the modern world have confronted the need to adapt themselves in some respect to the demands of the larger society and to the challenges posed by new ideologies and economic patterns. Jewish responses to these demands and challenges are best analyzed with the sociological concept of assimilation. The geographical and chronological parameters of the subject of gender and assimilation in modern Jewish history therefore

3. "Gender and Jewish History," Tikkun, Jan.–Feb. 1988, pp. 35–38; "Feminist Studies and Modern Jewish History," in Feminist Perspectives on Jewish Studies, ed. Lynn Davidman and Shelly Tenenbaum (New Haven: Yale University Press, in press).

coextend with modern Jewish history itself. Even "limiting" myself to Europe and the United States and focusing, with some exceptions, on the century 1850–1950, I have not exhausted the material relevant to the theme. Yet, the multinational comparisons I have drawn are sufficiently complicated to justify some significant omissions. In focusing on Europe and America, I necessarily defined as outside the concerns of this book the experience of ḥalutzot (women pioneers) in the prestate yishuv (Jewish society in Palestine) and their struggles to realize the equality that Zionism seemed to promise them. Likewise, I could not include the adaptation of the Jews of North Africa and the Middle East to Western culture through their contact with colonial regimes or with the educational institutions of the Alliance Israélite Universelle. The stories of the ḥalutzot and of Sephardi Jewry are compelling; no consideration of gender and assimilation in modern Jewish history is complete without them. I hope that colleagues with greater expertise in these areas than I have achieved will continue the important work that has begun in these areas.

As I pursued my research and writing, I decided that I could legitimately simplify my narrative by focusing on the distinction between Jews whose assimilation occurred within western and central Europe and the United States and those whose assimilation took place in the different conditions of eastern Europe. True, there were significant variations in the political, economic, and cultural development of Germany, France, England, and the United States. Yet, there were sufficient common features among these countries and their Jewish communities to allow for generalizations about a "Western model" of gender and assimilation. All of the Western nations offered some degree of civic equality to their Jewish populations and developed similar concepts of middle-class gender roles. By the last third of the nineteenth century, as a result of acculturation and upward social mobility, all of their relatively small Jewish communities were generally defined by their middle-class characteristics. Despite changes in women's actual social roles, the prescriptive power of the Western model prevailed at least until the middle of the current century. The Western model differed from what I define as the Eastern model of gender and assimilation. The latter derived from the political and cultural environment of multiethnic east European states that rejected Western-derived notions of civic equality. These states contained relatively large, and overwhelmingly non-middle-class, Jewish populations that retained such significant markers of distinctiveness as the Yiddish language and aspects of traditional Judaism. Because of their different environments and positions in their respective societies, "Western" and "Eastern" Jews constructed alternative versions of Jewish identity and approached gender roles and their relation to assimilation in distinguishable ways.

After analyzing the gendered processes of assimilation, and the representations of women that accompanied assimilation, in Western and Eastern societies, I turn to those Jews who brought together the two models in their own experience of assimilation: the eastern European Jewish immigrants who established large Jewish communities in the countries of the West, particularly the United States. Challenging elements of the Western model that rigidly limited the public role of women and spiritualized them as mothers, eastern European immigrants and their children contested the boundaries between domestic and public life that characterized middle-class gender norms. As they integrated into middle-class American culture, however, immigrant Jewish men and their sons—

like their predecessors in Western societies—played out their ambivalence about their own identity as Jews in non-Jewish societies in gendered terms. Jewish men represented Jewish women as responsible for the burdens of Jewishness they had to bear.

Among these burdens was the conflation of Jewishness and femininity in Western societies, with the consequent anxiety of Jewish men about their own masculinity. The last chapter investigates the effect of the association of Jews with the weaknesses commonly attributed to women upon some segments of the Jewish community. The book concludes that the gendered differences in the experience of assimilation and the growing representation of women as the primary transmitters of Jewish culture shaped modern Jewish identity on the battleground of sexual politics.

# I

# Paradoxes of Assimilation

"All of us who were still children thirty years ago can testify to
the incredible changes that have occurred both within us and
outside us. We have traversed, or better still, flown through
a thousand-year history."[1] So stated the German Jewish historian Isaak Markus Jost in 1833 in a public letter to a hostile
Prussian bureaucrat. Jost took pride in the great strides that
his Jewish contemporaries had taken in moving, as it were,
from the Jewish "Middle Ages" into the German "Modern
Age." Their efforts to assimilate economically, culturally, and
psychologically, he asserted, deserved approbation and support.

In presenting Jewish assimilation as a rapid and quasi-
miraculous journey of self-transformation, Jost articulated the
view of the Jewish intellectual elite, who embraced the possibilities of civic equality and social and cultural integration
offered by the Enlightenment and nineteenth-century political liberalism. Assimilation quickly became the central ongoing issue of debate within Jewish communities in the modern period. First promoted by both progressive Jewish leaders
and Christian supporters of Jewish emancipation (the con-
ferral of civic rights), it was later decried by Zionist activists
and Orthodox spokesmen as a betrayal of the Jewish people
and of Jewish tradition. "Assimilationist" became an epithet

1. Isaak Markus Jost, as cited by Ismar Schorsch, "From Wolfenbüttel
to Wissenschaft: The Divergent Paths of Isaak Markus Jost and Leopold
Zunz," *Leo Baeck Institute Yearbook* 22 (1977): 110.

of opprobrium. It has not been easy even for scholars of the Jewish past to explore the varieties and meanings of Jewish assimilation in the last two centuries in a nonpolemical way, although recently a sympathetic understanding of the ideology and identity of assimilated Jews has emerged, particularly among Jewish historians in America but also among some scholars in Israel. A number of historians have suggested that the blunt term "assimilation" obscures the varieties of behavior and the nuances of identity that characterize modern Jewry. The term "assimilation" often does not convey the multiple influences that together forge individual as well as collective identity, the different social contexts in which various aspects of identity are expressed, or the coexistence of the desire for full civic integration with the retention of what we might today call ethnic particularism.[2] With that caveat in mind, I will use the term "assimilation" in this study because both proponents and opponents of the accommodation of

2. On the mutual compatibility of assimilation and retention of Jewish identity, see Uriel Tal, *Christians and Jews in Germany: Religion, Politics, and Ideology in the Second Reich, 1870–1914*, trans. Noah Jonathan Jacobs (Ithaca: Cornell University Press, 1975). On the potential for multiple identities, see Gary Cohen, "Jews in German Society: Prague, 1860–1914," in *Jews and Germans from 1860 to 1933: The Problematic Symbiosis*, ed. David Bronsen (Heidelberg: Carl Winter Universitätsverlag, 1979), pp. 306–37. On the ethnic component of nineteenth-century French Jewish identity, see Phyllis Cohen Albert, "Ethnicity and Solidarity in Nineteenth-Century France," in *Mystics, Philosophers, and Politicians: Essays in Jewish Intellectual History in Honor of Alexander Altmann*, ed. Jehuda Reinharz and Daniel Swetschinski (Durham, N.C.: Duke University Press, 1982), pp. 249–74, and Phyllis Cohen Albert, "L'intégration et la persistance de l'ethnicité chez les Juifs dans la France moderne," in *Histoire politique des Juifs de France*, ed. Pierre Birnbaum (Paris: Presses de la Fondation Nationale des Sciences Politiques, 1990), pp. 221–43.

Jews to the norms of the non-Jewish societies in which they have lived have accepted it.

Historians have described the processes of assimilation of modern Jews as rapid and disruptive—causing a traumatic break with the past. Yet conclusions about the pace and extent of Jewish assimilation in the century of emancipation derive almost exclusively from scholarly investigation of the public behavior and pronouncements of a select group of urban Jewish men.[3] The experiences of Jewish women, and the contradiction between those experiences and the representation of women in expressions of Jewish public opinion, mandate a rethinking of the nature and significance of assimilation in the first generations of emancipation and into the contemporary period. I have chosen to focus on issues of gender because they not only highlight the regularly overlooked experiences of women but also pose new questions about male behavior. Gender is the socially and hierarchically constructed division of the sexes—or, in the words of historian Joan Wallach Scott, "a constitutive element of social relationships based on perceived differences between the sexes."[4] Considerations of

3. A notable exception is the work of Marion Kaplan: "Tradition and Transition: The Acculturation, Assimilation and Integration of Jews in Imperial Germany—A Gender Analysis," *Leo Baeck Institute Yearbook* 27 (1982): 3–35; "Priestess and Hausfrau: Women and Tradition in the German-Jewish Family," in *The Jewish Family: Myths and Reality*, ed. Steven M. Cohen and Paula E. Hyman (New York: Holmes & Meier, 1986), pp. 62–81; *The Making of the Jewish Middle Class: Women, Family, and Identity in Imperial Germany* (New York: Oxford University Press, 1991); and *The Jewish Feminist Movement in Germany: The Campaigns of the Jüdischer Frauenbund, 1904–1938* (Westport, Conn.: Greenwood Press, 1979).

4. For an extended theoretical consideration of gender in historical research as well as historical case studies, see Joan Wallach Scott, *Gender and the Politics of History* (New York: Columbia University Press, 1988).

gender can reshape our understanding of both assimilation in modern Jewish history and the meanings that Jews have attached to assimilation.

To assess assimilation and its impact upon modern Jewry in Europe and America, we must distinguish between assimilation as a sociological process and assimilation as a project. As a *sociological process*, assimilation consists of several different stages. The first steps, often called acculturation, include the acquisition of the basic markers of the larger society, such as language, dress, and the more amorphous category of "values." The integration of minority-group members into the majority institutions follows, with the attendant weakening of minority institutions. The end point of assimilation is the dissolution of the minority by biological merger with the majority through intermarriage. For assimilation to proceed to its last stages, two mutually reinforcing factors must be present: the desire of the minority to become like and to join the majority and the receptivity of the majority to the participation of minority-group members in its midst. Without openness on the part of the larger society, it is possible for a minority to be fully acculturated and yet remain poorly integrated.[5]

The acculturation of nineteenth-century Jews, especially in western and central Europe and the United States, to the language, dress, and mores of the Gentile middle classes of

5. For an elaboration of a sociological interpretation of assimilation, see Milton Gordon, *Assimilation in American Life: The Role of Race, Religion and National Origins* (New York: Oxford University Press, 1964). This work has had an enormous influence on modern Jewish historians, especially those educated in the United States. For one of the first studies sensitive to the distinction between acculturation and integration, see Todd Endelman, *The Jews of Georgian England: Tradition and Change in a Liberal Society* (Philadelphia: Jewish Publication Society, 1979).

their surroundings constituted a break (at first, nonideological) with a traditional Jewish mentality that had defined the Gentile as wholly Other. It also reflected an eagerness of the Jewish elites and then the masses to take advantage of the new economic, social, and cultural opportunities made available by Enlightenment humanism and the expansion of political rights. The process of assimilation also bespoke a new openness on the part of European and American elites to Jews as potential legal and social equals. As a process, then, assimilation may be divided into two components: acculturation, which depends on the behavior of the minority, and integration, which demands changed attitudes and behavior on the part of members of minority and majority alike.

As a project, assimilation was the official response of Jewish communal leaders in both Europe and the United States to emancipation and was expressed in communal policy. In the last quarter of the eighteenth century, emancipation was placed on the general public agenda, but it took more than a century for the Jews of the various western and central European countries as well as the United States to secure fully equal political rights. (The vast majority of European Jews, those living in the Russian Empire, were not accorded equal citizenship until the 1917 Russian Revolution, and as we shall see in the following chapter, the dynamics of assimilation were quite different there.) Because of the intense interest in the "Jewish question" and particularly the debates surrounding the first emancipation of Jews in France during the French Revolution, Jewish leaders understood that citizenship was conferred with the explicit expectation that Jews would become like their fellow countrymen. Both those who favored and those who opposed Jewish emancipation at the end of the eighteenth century looked askance at contemporary evidence of Jewish economic and cultural particularity, which they described as moral and cultural debasement. Opponents of emancipation saw this particularity as inherent in Judaism or in the Jews. Emancipation should be deferred until Jews had changed, they argued. Proponents of Jewish emancipation, on the other hand, predicted that emancipation would lead to a thoroughgoing improvement in Jewish behavior because the alleged defects of the Jews, such as their superstitiousness and their dishonesty, resulted from persecution. Bring an end to persecution and Jewish behavior would automatically be transformed, they argued. As one writer of the French Enlightenment confidently put it in 1788, "we can make of the Jews what we want them to become."[6] With the cessation of legal discrimination and of restrictions on Jewish economic activity and the elimination of Jewish communal autonomy and self-government, the Jews would assimilate to their neighbors, differing from them only in the matter of their creed.

Without exception Jews of western and central Europe and the United States publicly accepted emancipation and welcomed the possibilities it offered, including opportunities for acculturation and social integration. One French Jewish communal leader, for example, took the occasion of the emancipation decree of 1791 to call upon his fellow Jews to help realize an idyllic future of social harmony, in part by sending their children to public schools: "Through this union in the schools, our children, as well as those of our fellow citizens, will note from their tender youth that neither opinion

6. [Adolphe] Thiéry, *Dissertation sur cette question: Est-il des moyens de rendre les Juifs plus heureux et plus utiles en France?* (Paris, 1788), p. 66; reprinted in facsimile in *La Révolution française et l'émancipation des Juifs* (Paris: Editions d'Histoire Sociale, 1968), vol. 2.

nor religious difference prevents fraternal love."[7] For the most part, Jewish voices dissenting from this expectation of the easy attainment of fraternity would not be heard until the end of the nineteenth century. Throughout the nineteenth century the male Jewish elites who controlled Jewish communal institutions, and who were generally recruited from among the prosperous and the acculturated, exhorted their less upwardly mobile constituents to demonstrate either that the faith of the proponents of emancipation had not been misplaced (in the case where civic rights had already been granted) or that the Jews were now worthy of equal rights (in the numerous cases where emancipation had been partial or deferred).

Yet the Jewish project of assimilation differed somewhat from the Enlightenment version. Although Jewish spokesmen forecast a harmonious future of equality, they did not intend to disappear as a recognizable group into a homogeneous national society. In that respect they dissented from the hopes of many Gentile proponents of Jewish emancipation. As the historian Uriel Tal (and others subsequently) has pointed out, Jewish leaders defined the goals of assimilation as the acculturation and social integration of the Jews, ideally into the bourgeoisie, along with the retention of some form of Jewish identity based upon a shared religious culture and memory.[8] They encouraged acculturation and the shedding

7. Berr Isaac Berr, "Lettre d'un citoyen, membre de la ci-devant Communauté des Juifs de Lorraine, à ses confrères, à l'occasion du droit du Citoyen actif, rendu aux Juifs par le décret du 28 septembre 1791" (Nancy, 1791); reprinted in *La Révolution française et l'émancipation des Juifs* (Paris: Editions d'Histoire Sociale, 1968), 8:16–17.
8. See the sources cited in n. 2.

of external markers of Jewishness but supported religious, educational, and philanthropic institutions that would maintain a sense of Jewish particularism within the larger society. Denying the possibility of conflict between religious and civic obligations, they also presumed that successful completion of this project of assimilation would eliminate the last vestiges of social prejudice against Jews.

The historiography of modern Jewry has documented the relatively rapid acculturation of the Jews of nineteenth-century western and central Europe and the United States along with their impressive upward social mobility. I will begin my exploration of the interplay of gender and assimilation by addressing the experience of these Western Jews because they became the model, for good and bad, of assimilation. They also defined the problems associated with both the process and the project of assimilation. To be sure, village and small-town Jews in western and central Europe initially resisted assimilation and maintained their traditional religious and economic patterns for several generations after the promise or reality of emancipation had transformed the culture and socioeconomic structure of their more urbanized kin. Local political and social contexts shaped a multiplicity of social and cultural patterns even among Jews of the West, who had been most affected by Enlightenment and emancipation. By the last quarter of the nineteenth century, however, the majority of western and central European and American Jews were city dwellers, assimilated in language and comportment into the local middle classes and succeeding as players in the capitalist economy. In the German states, for example, at the beginning of the nineteenth century, Jews were poorer than their fellow countrymen, paying a disproportionately low share of taxes; by the end of the century, their higher tax contributions indicate they were more prosperous than other Germans.[9] Taking advantage of educational opportunities, impressive numbers of Jewish men became doctors and lawyers. And, as is well known, in such major European centers as Paris, Berlin, and especially Vienna, Jews exerted a considerable influence as creators, critics, and consumers of high culture. Middle-class Jews thronged the concert halls and art galleries and regularly purchased the liberal newspapers, among whose editors and writers Jews figured prominently.[10] The assimilation of Jews in Western societies in the past two centuries and the forging of a modern Jewish identity cannot be separated from the middle-class context in which these processes were embedded.

Jewish women assimilated along with their male kin, but they did so in different frameworks. The examination of women's experiences reveals how gender shapes the process of assimilation. In the nineteenth century in western and central Europe and in the United States, whose Jewish population then derived primarily from central Europe, Jewish women's gender limited their assimilation by confining them, like other middle-class women, to the domestic scene and thereby re-

9. Jacob Toury, "Der Eintritt der Juden ins deutsche Bürgertum," in *Das Judentum in der deutschen Umwelt, 1800–1850*, ed. Hans Liebeschütz and Arnold Paucker (Tübingen: Mohr, 1977), pp. 139–242.

10. See Michael Marrus, *The Politics of Assimilation: A Study of the French Jewish Community at the Time of the Dreyfus Affair* (New York: Oxford University Press, 1971), pp. 35–45; Marsha Rozenblit, *The Jews of Vienna, 1867–1914: Assimilation and Community* (Albany: State University of New York Press, 1983), pp. 1–2; Steven Beller, *Vienna and the Jews, 1867–1938: A Cultural History* (Cambridge: Cambridge University Press, 1989); Robert S. Wistrich, *The Jews of Vienna in the Age of Franz Joseph* (Oxford: Oxford University Press, 1989); Calvin Goldscheider and Alan Zuckerman, *The Transformation of the Jews* (Chicago: University of Chicago Press, 1984), pp. 44–49, 85–90.

stricting their opportunities for education and participation in the public realm of economy and civic life. Unlike their brothers and husbands, middle-class Jewish women in Western societies confronted neither the workplace nor, until the twentieth century, the university. Because their social life occurred within their domestic context and the religiously segmented philanthropic associations considered appropriate for women of their class, they initially had fewer contacts with non-Jews and experienced fewer external challenges to their childhood culture than did Jewish men.[11] Although the twentieth century offered new educational and employment opportunities for women, gender divisions and presumptions of appropriate female behavior that had developed in the nineteenth century retained much of their power, only gradually succumbing to the blurring of the boundaries between domestic and public realms. For most of the modern period, then, Jewish women display fewer signs of radical assimilation than men.

If one examines statistics on the most-extreme manifestations of assimilation—that is, intermarriage and conversion— Jewish women throughout the Western world have "lagged behind" their brothers until the present day.[12] In Germany, to give but one example, between 1873 and 1882 only 7 percent of all Jewish converts were women. Moreover, men and women seem to have converted for different purposes: women, primarily to join with a non-Jew in marriage, their

11. I am relying here on the analysis of Marion Kaplan found in her "Tradition and Transition," and "Priestess and Hausfrau," as well as in her book *The Making of the Jewish Middle Class*.

12. Todd M. Endelman, "Introduction," in *Jewish Apostasy in the Modern World*, ed. Todd M. Endelman (New York: Holmes & Meier, 1987), p. 13.

main vehicle of social survival and upward mobility; men, primarily to overcome obstacles to their professional advancement. Although both men and women converted to obtain social mobility, the gender division of public and domestic spheres determined the nature and timing of their decisions about radical assimilation. Only as lower-middle-class Jewish women entered the workforce in increasing numbers at the turn of the twentieth century and thereby had increasing contact both with non-Jews and with antisemitism did the proportion of female Jewish converts rise. Yet, at 37 percent of Jewish converts in Germany in 1908 and 40 percent in 1912, the conversion rate of Jewish women still remained substantially below that of men.[13]

Among Western Jewish communities of the modern period, there is only one exception to the generalization about women's lower rates of intermarriage and conversion. In Berlin in the years between 1770 and 1799, 60 percent of the 249 Jews who converted to another faith were women, and as the rate of conversion zoomed in the following decade, women again took the lead.[14] Most prominent among these women was a small coterie of some two dozen women generally referred to as the "salon Jewesses." Celebrated as witty and charming, they took advantage of a short-lived, Romantically inspired openness on the part of intellectuals and penurious nobility to the company of wealthy and cultivated Jewish women to make their mark in society and to enter into socially advantageous marriages with non-Jews (conversion

13. Todd M. Endelman, "The Social and Political Context of Conversion in Germany and England," in ibid., p. 90.
14. Deborah Hertz, "Seductive Conversion in Berlin, 1770–1809," in ibid., pp. 58, 64, 67.

was necessary because civil marriage did not exist). Dorothea Mendelssohn, Henrietta Herz, Rahel Varnhagen, and their fellow salon Jewesses temporarily found in Berlin literary "high society" a celebrity impossible in Jewish society, where entertainment was largely gender-segregated and women's role as hostess and muse was neither developed nor admired.[15]

Despite the anomaly of their situation, the salon Jewesses have most often been discussed not in terms of their specific social and cultural context but as paradigmatic of Jewish women's experience as they confronted modernity. Such fine historians as Michael Meyer and Jacob Katz have suggested that the salon Jewesses typify the vulnerability of Jewish women to the blandishments of secular Western culture because of the failure of the Jewish community to provide them with any significant Jewish education.[16] For most Western Jewish women, however, this argument is not borne out by evidence, for, as the historian Deborah Hertz has shown, the salon Jewesses deviated significantly from the experience of other Jewish women.[17]

Among the vast majority of Jews who neither converted nor intermarried, there does appear to have been a significant gender difference in Jewish practice and identity—but in the opposite direction from the example of the salon Jewesses. Marion Kaplan's history of middle-class Jewish women in Imperial Germany, for example, persuasively demonstrates that

15. For a compelling analysis of this group and their social context, see Deborah Hertz, *Jewish High Society in Old Regime Berlin* (New Haven: Yale University Press, 1988).

16. Michael A. Meyer, *The Origins of the Modern Jew* (Detroit: Wayne State University Press, 1967), pp. 85–114; Jacob Katz, *Out of the Ghetto* (Cambridge: Harvard University Press, 1973), pp. 56, 120.

17. Hertz, *Jewish High Society in Old Regime Berlin*.

the same men who absented themselves from the synagogue and who saw themselves, and have been described in the historical literature, as thoroughly assimilated—indeed as prototypical assimilated Jews—lived in families where their wives continued to take cognizance of the Jewish calendar and its rituals. This occurred even as the traditional observance of many public practices waned among central European Jews.[18] The dispute between Sigmund Freud and his wife, Martha, over the lighting of Sabbath candles is, therefore, not idiosyncratic but representative of a widespread gendered difference in attitudes toward religious tradition.[19] Most Jewish women seem to have been eager to maintain Jewish rituals within the home, the domain that fell under their jurisdiction, and unlike Martha Bernays Freud, most seem to have prevailed. The rich collection of German Jewish memoirs and diaries from the late nineteenth and early twentieth centuries, written largely by men, includes numerous assessments of the family as nonreligious and assimilated while mentioning in passing that mothers taught their children Jewish prayers or even prayed regularly at home. Women seem to have persisted in ritual observance even after their husbands had abandoned these practices. A German Jewish woman born in 1862, for example, recounted sardonically in her memoirs that her mother fasted and prayed on Yom Kippur whereas her father found it "easier to fast after a hearty breakfast."[20]

In Victorian England, where the Anglo-Jewish elite encoun-

---

18. Kaplan, *The Making of the Jewish Middle Class*, pp. 69–84.

19. For an account of this dispute, see Peter Gay, *Freud: A Life for Our Time* (New Haven: Yale University Press, 1988), p. 54.

20. Anna Kronthal, *Posner Mübekuchen: Jugend Erinnerungen einer Posnerin* (Munich, 1932), p. 27, as cited in Kaplan, "Priestess and Hausfrau," p. 71.

tered little discrimination and felt comfortable with a modest display of religiosity, Jewish women of the upper classes expressed a religious sensibility that was considered appropriate to their social class. Indeed, Todd Endelman has found that, as among assimilated central European Jews, "[t]he wives and daughters of communal magnates appear to have been more concerned with spiritual matters" than were their male kin.[21] Thus, the wife and children of the liberal politician Viscount Herbert Samuel regularly attended Sabbath services, while he limited his synagogue participation to the High Holidays. Although Samuel abandoned the traditional Judaism of his youth after losing his faith while at Balliol College, Beatrice Franklin Samuel did succeed in persuading her husband to refrain from working or traveling on the Sabbath.[22]

The inclusion of gender in the study of Jewish assimilation thus introduces for consideration the domestic realm, which has tended to disappear from historical view. Given the privatization of much of Jewish behavior in the wake of emancipation, historians must enter the Jewish home to assess the nature of Jewish assimilation. To do so, they have to work assiduously and creatively, mining resources like memoirs, diaries, personal correspondence, and material culture to bridge the division of public and private spheres and to explore the tensions between public and private selves. To offer just one suggestive example: A recent museum exhibition on the Dreyfus Affair included in the section on the Dreyfus family a decorative cloth that had been displayed on the

21. Todd M. Endelman, Radical Assimilation in English Jewish History, 1656–1945 (Bloomington: Indiana University Press, 1990), pp. 81–85. The quotation is from p. 84.

22. Ibid., p. 82.

wall in the Dreyfus home.[23] What does it signify when a highly assimilated Jewish family, often depicted as alienated from the Jewish community and Jewish tradition, chooses to display a cloth visually celebrating the three pilgrimage holidays of Passover, Pentecost, and Tabernacles? Surely it suggests a more complex identity as assimilated French Jews than we might have previously imagined.[24]

The persistence of Jewish ritual and of the expression of religiosity among Jewish women in assimilated families, as well as phenomena like the Dreyfuses' interior decor, illustrates how attention to gender and to domestic life challenges conventional views of assimilation. Gendered difference in religious behavior was by no means limited to the European scene in the second half of the nineteenth century. Considerable evidence of a similar gender division in religious practice exists among second- and third-generation Jewish families of central European origin in America. By the end of the nineteenth century commentators allude to the "feminization" of the synagogue, a phenomenon parallel to the feminization of the Protestant churches described by a number of historians. Typical is an 1897 remark of one Jewish woman, who wrote of Reform synagogues of the time, that "year in and year out, for many long years, . . . [the rabbis'] efforts in sermon and lec-

---

23. For the decorative cloth, see Norman Kleeblatt, ed., *The Dreyfus Affair: Art, Truth, Justice* (Berkeley: University of California Press, 1987), p. 271.

24. Pierre Birnbaum has documented that the affirmation of Jewish identity and the practice of endogamy were common among Jews who made careers as servants of the French state, whether in the army or the civil administration. See his *Les fous de la République: Histoire politique des Juifs d'Etat de Gambetta à Vichy* (Paris: Arthème Fayard, 1992).

ture have been prepared for and delivered to congregational audiences composed almost exclusively of women."[25]

This depiction of the greater retention of Jewish ritual observance by middle-class Jewish women than by their male kin is not intended to suggest that women were by nature more loyal than men to Jewish tradition. Rather, it points to the fact that middle-class gender norms of behavior eroded traditional patterns of Jewish practice among men while facilitating a measure of Jewish ritual observance among women. The comparatively high degree of religiosity of assimilated Jewish women is thus, in itself, a female form of the project of assimilation. By the middle of the nineteenth century western Jews had adapted themselves, and their Judaism, to the prevailing bourgeois model of female domesticity, the so-called cult of domesticity. This ideology called upon women to create a peaceful domestic environment free from the stresses of the larger society and devoted to the preservation and transmission of traditional morality, while men assumed the burden of earning a living and governing society. Religion fell naturally within women's domain, for it drew upon emotion to disseminate morality and fortify social order. Modern men were considered too busy with worldly concerns to assume

25. Faith Rogow, *Gone to Another Meeting: The National Council of Jewish Women, 1893–1993* (Tuscaloosa: University of Alabama Press, 1993), pp. 47–49. The quotation (from Theresa Lesem writing in the *Reform Advocate,* 27 Mar. 1897, p. 90) appears on p. 47. On the feminization of American Christianity, see Ann Douglas, *The Feminization of American Culture* (New York: Knopf, 1977), Barbara Welter, "The Cult of True Womanhood," *American Quarterly* 18 (1966): 151–74, and Barbara Welter, "The Feminization of American Religion: 1800–1860," in *Clio's Consciousness Raised,* ed. Mary Hartman and Lois Banner (New York: Harper, 1973), pp. 137–55.

this task. Bourgeois culture thus expected women to be at least moderately religious, certainly more religious than men, since they were deemed inherently more spiritual. The bourgeois division of labor between the sexes also conferred responsibility upon women for religiously based "good works," including the basic religious education of children. Although traditional Judaism had also recognized women's spirituality, it had reserved to men the premier manifestation of religious piety: the intensive study of sacred texts. When life in the modern Western world led most assimilating Jewish men to abandon traditional Jewish culture and limit their religious expression to periodic appearances at synagogue and the performance of some communal service, their wives absorbed the dominant societal expectations of women as the guardians of religion.

Bourgeois culture also linked religious expression to familial sentiment. Because so much of Jewish religious ritual is home centered, it was relatively easy for women to meet bourgeois norms. There was less dissonance between Jewish religious practice and women's daily routines than was the case for men, whose traditional Jewish role was centered in public ritual in the synagogue or house of study. By retaining some domestic aspects of Jewish tradition, including customary foods, and transforming others into ostensibly secular family celebrations, such as the Friday evening, rather than Sunday, dinner, Jewish women fulfilled their prescriptive role and transmitted what the anthropologist Barbara Myerhoff, in a very different setting, called "domestic Judaism."[26] The

26. Barbara Myerhoff, *Number Our Days* (New York: E. P. Dutton, 1978), pp. 232–68.

general norms of bourgeois society thus reinforced the retention by women of domestic Jewish ritual practice while undermining ritual observance for men.

Men and women alike within Western Jewish communities adopted the dominant middle-class view that women were responsible for inculcating moral and religious consciousness in their children and within the home more generally. According to this view, women were also the primary factor in the formation of their children's Jewish identity. The conservative role of maternal keeper of the domestic flame of Judaism became a fundamental aspect of the project of assimilation. In the countries of the West, the Jewish press, which emerged in the middle of the nineteenth century, frequently expressed this concept of women's centrality in maintaining the home as the primary site of Jewish sensibility and in transmitting Jewish culture and identity. Interestingly, although women's roles expanded by the end of the nineteenth century, the rhetoric of the true Jewish woman whose role it was to preside over the domestic sphere, ministering to the spiritual health of her family and thereby strengthening the Jewish community, continued unabated.

As early as 1844 the London *Jewish Chronicle* commented that because Jewish youth were "externally restrained by political hindrance and by allurements of apostasy . . . [they] require *especial and particular maternal vigilance and attendance.*"[27] Similarly, in 1852 the *Archives israélites*, the journal representing progressive Jewish thought in France, depicted a bourgeois Jewish family where gender roles were highly differentiated and where the socialization of its children depended upon the mother:

27. Jewish Chronicle 1 (1844–45): 55, emphasis mine.

Our fathers, absorbed by their business, their commerce, their industry, their travels, . . . cannot follow with a vigilant eye the physical, moral, and intellectual progress of the young family; they abandon that care to maternal solicitude. The woman is the guardian angel of the house; . . . her religiosity, her virtues, are a living example for the children, whom she has constantly under her eyes.

The journal concluded, "Man exists for public life; woman, for domestic life."[28]

The German Jewish press also waxed eloquent about the role of women within their proper sphere. One newspaper in 1895 went so far as to call "the Hausfrau" "a priestess of the home."[29] American Jewish leaders shared this assessment of women's nature, stressing the long-standing historical role of Jewish women within the home. In 1835 Isaac Leeser, an important leader and later publisher of the newspaper the Occident, declared, in a sermon that proclaimed the inappropriateness of serious education for women, that a woman's "home should be the place of her actions; there her influence should be felt, to soothe, to calm, to sanctify, to render happy the rugged career of a father, a brother, a husband, or a child."[30] Within a generation the shapers of American Jewish public opinion included a specifically Jewish component to the Jewish woman's domestic role: the "Mother in Israel," a Jewish version of the American "True Woman." In 1876 the editor of a traditionalist Jewish newspaper, the Jewish Messenger,

28. Archives israélites 13 (1852): 612.

29. As cited in Kaplan, "Priestess and Hausfrau," pp. 62, 77 n.

30. Isaac Leeser, "How to Educate Jewish Girls," as cited in The American Jewish Woman: A Documentary History, ed. Jacob Rader Marcus (New York and Cincinnati: Ktav Publishing House and American Jewish Archives, 1981), p. 130.

asserted: "The women of Israel have at all times been the conservators of our hallowed creed."[31] The very same year that the German housewife was dubbed a priestess, prominent Reform rabbi Emil Hirsch described her American counterpart as a "Priestess of the Jewish ideal, Prophetess of Purity and Refinement."[32] His colleague in the Reform rabbinate Kaufmann Kohler used the pages of the *American Hebrew* at about the same time to call upon Jewish women in a similar vein to become "the standard-bearer[s] of religion," who would "give us again Jewish homes, . . . a Judaism spiritualized."[33] In recognition of women's important role as the first (and sometimes only) Jewish teachers of their children, Jewish communal leaders began to emphasize the importance of providing sufficient Jewish education to girls to enable them to carry out their destined maternal responsibilities. As the *Archives israélites* put it in 1852, "[T]he health of our religion depends henceforth above all on the education of girls."[34]

Although Jewish women in the West, who had encountered the challenges of secular culture, accommodated to prevail-

31. Abram S. Isaacs, "Our Daughters," *Jewish Messenger* 39, no. 12 (1876): 4, as cited in Diane Lichtenstein, *Writing Their Nations: The Tradition of Nineteenth-Century American Jewish Women Writers* (Bloomington: Indiana University Press, 1992), p. 29 (on the Mother in Israel trope, see pp. 23–31).

32. *American Jewess* 1, no. 1 (Apr. 1895): 11, as cited in Jenna Weissman Joselit, *New York's Jewish Jews: The Orthodox Community in the Interwar Years* (Bloomington: Indiana University Press, 1990), p. 97.

33. *American Hebrew*, 23 Mar. 1894, p. 621. Karla Goldman points out that Kaufmann Kohler's views on women's domestic role remained nearly unchanged over a period of some fifty years. See her "The Ambivalence of Reform Judaism: Kaufmann Kohler and the Ideal Jewish Woman," *American Jewish History* 79, no. 4 (1990): 477–99, esp. 484, 497.

34. *Archives israélites* 13 (1852): 612.

ing expectations of the middle-class woman's position in the home, they also reshaped the boundaries between the domestic and the public spheres and thereby assumed an expanded role within the Jewish community.[35] The female version of the project of Jewish assimilation contained potentially radical elements in addition to its conservative domestic thrust. Middle-class Jewish women in Western societies, particularly in the United States, happily claimed the new definitions of female responsibility for religious socialization of the young and for care of society's unfortunates. Drawing on these gender norms, and later on the ideology of domestic feminism that conceptualized society as merely the domestic realm writ large, they developed new forms of female Jewish expression. Subsequently, they began to demand communal recognition of their public roles.

In the small, new Jewish communities of nineteenth-century America, whose members were more highly integrated within the larger society socially than within any other contemporary locale, middle- and upper-class women adopted the prevailing American concept that charity was woman's work. At the same time they expanded the philanthropic activity that Jewish women had conducted in ḥevrot (associations) in the traditional Jewish community. Nearly every Jewish community of moderate size sustained a Hebrew Ladies' Benevolent Society.[36] In Philadelphia, for example, in

35. On the shifting of boundaries between public and private, see Beth Wenger, "Jewish Women and Voluntarism: Beyond the Myth of Enablers," *American Jewish History* 79, no. 1 (1989): 16–36.

36. For primary sources on Hebrew Ladies' Benevolent Societies in Hartford, Anniston (Alabama), Portsmouth (Ohio), Galveston, and Philadelphia, see Marcus, ed., *The American Jewish Woman*, pp. 204–22. On the Hebrew Ladies' Benevolent Society of Atlanta, founded in 1870, see Beth

1819 the renowned Rebecca Gratz along with several other women who worshiped in the city's premier synagogue, Mikveh Israel, established the Female Hebrew Benevolent Society. Its volunteers organized home relief and eventually medical care for the local Jewish poor, an employment bureau for women and children, and a traveler's aid society. Some twenty years later, in 1838, women active in the Female Hebrew Benevolent Society founded the first Hebrew Sunday School in the United States, which became a model for the many others that followed.[37] The women who dedicated themselves to philanthropic and educational work among their fellow Jews defined their activity in moral and religious terms. Although they were influenced by Christian models of female philanthropy, they saw their efforts as a safeguard against Christian missionaries who knocked on the doors of poor Jews to offer assistance accompanied by proselytizing. Jewish female activists enjoyed the possibilities for sociability that voluntarism offered them as well as opportunities for demonstrating their skills beyond the confines of their homes.

Similar concepts of female duties and possibilities for self-expression led Jewish women in western and central Europe to express their maternal roles in social institutions dedicated to caring for the Jewish poor and to providing Jewish education. In the small Jewish community of England, Louise

Wenger, "The Southern Lady and the Jewish Woman: The Early Organizational Life of Atlanta's Jewish Women" (senior honors thesis, Wesleyan University, 1985), pp. 23–24.

37. Evelyn Bodek, " 'Making Do': Jewish Women and Philanthropy," in *Jewish Life in Philadelphia*, ed. Murray Friedman (Philadelphia: ISHI Publications, 1983), pp. 145–47. See also Linda Gordon Kuzmack, *Woman's Cause: The Jewish Women's Movement in England and the United States, 1881–1933* (Columbus: Ohio State University Press, 1990), pp. 20–22.

Rothschild played a role similar to Rebecca Gratz's, founding the Jewish Ladies' Benevolent Loan Society and the Ladies' Visiting Society in London in 1840. She also helped to administer the Jews' Free School, a communal elementary school. Rothschild and her fellow volunteers, like Jewish women in the United States, combined traditional Jewish patterns of charity (*zedakah*) with the new forms of denominational philanthropy conducted by Christian women.[38] In nineteenth-century Germany, on the other hand, Jewish women initially conducted their charitable work along more-traditional lines. They doled out poor relief, cared for the female dead as they had for generations through the female *hevrah kadisha* (burial society), gathered money to provide dowries for poor brides, and administered funds to ensure that indigent Jews had the means to celebrate holidays. Gradually they also expanded their philanthropy, creating women's societies organized according to the latest concepts of "scientific charity" and concerned with the education of girls and the welfare of children. By the end of the nineteenth century their philanthropic activity enabled them to forge connections across confessional lines with other German women.[39] In France as well, Jewish women continued traditional forms of *zedakah* while engaging in the types of modern philanthropy conducted by bourgeois Catholic women.[40]

38. Kuzmack, *Woman's Cause*, pp. 10–12.

39. Kaplan, *The Jewish Feminist Movement in Germany*, pp. 67–68; Kaplan, "Tradition and Transition," p. 23; Kaplan, *The Making of the Jewish Middle Class*, pp. 192–227.

40. On Jewish women's philanthropy in nineteenth-century urban France, see my *The Emancipation of the Jews of Alsace: Acculturation and Tradition in the Nineteenth Century* (New Haven: Yale University Press, 1991), pp. 60–61. On the assumption by bourgeois Catholic women of increased responsi-

Although most Jewish women in the West expressed their Jewish sentiment primarily through private devotions in the home and sectarian philanthropy, there emerged a handful of exceptional individuals who saw it as their responsibility to use the written word to accomplish the defense of Judaism as well as the task of educating other Jewish women, who would then influence their children. They based their activity upon the modern expectation that women would serve as the primary inculcators of Jewish consciousness in children, just as Western bourgeois culture saw mothers as the first teachers of moral values to the younger generation.[41] In traditional Jewish society in eastern Europe in the eighteenth century a few women had composed tkhines, petitionary prayers in Yiddish intended for a female audience.[42] In central Europe and the United States in the nineteenth century, metaphorical descendants of Sarah bas Tovim and Sarah Rebecca Rachel

---

bility for charity, see Bonnie Smith, *Ladies of the Leisure Class: The Bourgeoises of Northern France in the Nineteenth Century* (Princeton: Princeton University Press, 1981), pp. 123–61.

41. In France, for example, the leaders of the Alliance Israélite Universelle focused upon moral education as the central goal in the schools it founded throughout the Levant. They saw educating female students for the task of rearing their children with the values of the European bourgeoisie as crucial to their efforts. See Aron Rodrigue, *French Jews, Turkish Jews: The Alliance Israélite Universelle and the Politics of Jewish Schooling in Turkey, 1860–1925* (Bloomington: Indiana University Press, 1990), pp. 78–79.

42. On tkhines and their function among Jewish women in the sixteenth through eighteenth centuries, see Chava Weissler, "Prayers in Yiddish and the Religious World of Ashkenazic Women," in *Jewish Women in Historical Perspective*, ed. Judith R. Baskin (Detroit: Wayne State University Press, 1991), pp. 159–81, and Chava Weissler, "Traditional Piety of Ashkenazic Women," in *Jewish Spirituality*, ed. Arthur Green (New York: Crossroad, 1987), 2:245–75.

Leah Horowitz, two authors of collections of *tkhines*, also wrote prayers in the vernacular (in German or English) and with a modern sensibility. The poet Penina Moise (1797–1880) of Charleston, South Carolina, composed the first American Jewish hymnal (and served, incidentally, as the director of Congregation Beth Elohim's Sunday School).[43] In 1855 Fanny Neuda (1819–1894), widow of one rabbi in Moravia and sister of another in Vienna, wrote a German prayer book for women. *Stunden der Andacht* (Hours of devotion) was so popular that by the 1920s it had gone through twenty-eight editions and had also been translated into English.[44]

The most prolific and influential of these Jewish women writers who addressed religious themes was England's Grace Aguilar (1816–1847), of Portuguese Marrano descent. In her short life of thirty-one years, she wrote a number of books about Judaism, in addition to novels, poems, and translations.[45] Apologetic in tone, they were designed to instill pride in Jewish readers and reinforce the faith of Jews fully at home in Western culture. Aguilar saw her role as defender of the faith against widely accepted Christian disparagement of Judaism. In her 1845 volume *The Women of Israel*, which surveyed Jewish history with particular attention to the biblical era, she

43. For a selection of Moise's poetry, see Marcus, ed., *The American Jewish Woman*, pp. 124–28, and Ellen M. Umansky and Dianne Ashton, eds., *Four Centuries of Jewish Women's Spirituality—A Sourcebook* (Boston: Beacon Press, 1992), pp. 88–90. For an analysis of Moise's work, see Lichtenstein, *Writing Their Nations*, pp. 71–74.

44. Fanny Neuda, *Stunden der Andacht* (1857; Prague: W. Pascheles, 1868). On Neuda, see the *Encyclopedia Judaica*, 12:1008.

45. On Grace Aguilar see Kuzmack, *Woman's Cause*, p. 15, and Montagu Frank Modder, *The Jew in the Literature of England* (Philadelphia: Jewish Publication Society, 1939), pp. 182–88.

was anxious to prove that the position of women in Judaism was higher than in any other culture. "[I]t is impossible to read the Mosaic law," she asserted, "without the true and touching conviction, that the female Hebrew was even more an object of the tender and soothing care of the Eternal than the male."[46]

Aguilar's defense of the high status of women within Jewish tradition, though intended to provide rationales for loyalty to Judaism, derived from assumptions about gender and assimilation widespread among acculturated Jews of her generation. In Aguilar's view, Jewish women had a special religious vocation, or "mission," "as witnesses of that faith which first raised, cherished, and defended them. . . . A religion of love is indeed necessary to woman, yet more so than to man."[47] Because of woman's natural spirituality, Aguilar urged the Jewish woman, in contradiction of traditional Jewish custom, to dedicate the gift of her "silvery voice and ear for harmony" not only to pleasing man but also to singing God's praises in his sanctuary as well as teaching songs of thanksgiving to her children at home.[48] In fact, Aguilar highlighted the role of Jewish women as teachers of their children. But rather than seeing this role as a recent addition to women's tasks, she asserted that its source was "our ancient fathers, whose opinion is evidently founded on our holy law."[49] "To the women of Israel, then," she concluded, "is intrusted the noble privilege of hastening 'the great and glorious day of the Lord,' by the instruction they bestow upon their sons, and the spiritual ele-

46. Grace Aguilar, The Women of Israel, 2 vols. in 1 (New York: D. Appleton & Co., 1851), p. 9.

47. Ibid., pp. 12–13.

48. Ibid., p. 152.

49. Ibid., p. 323. For other comments on women as the religious instructors of their children, see pp. 155, 157, 165.

vation to which they may attain in social intercourse, and yet more in domestic life."[50]

Aguilar's *The Women of Israel* suggests the double-edged implications of the bourgeois gender division that placed religion and the inculcation of religious sensibilities within the female domain. On the one hand, Aguilar manifested a strong loyalty to Jewish faith and to Jewish distinctiveness; she expressed a firm belief in woman's inherent religiosity as well as in her physical and mental inferiority to man—doctrines that we might label profoundly conservative. On the other hand, on the basis of her understanding of women's religious mission, she championed women's religious education and the ceremony of confirmation for both sexes—innovations we could rightly see as progressive.[51] In fact, she recognized the opportunities that her own time offered Jewish women, and she concluded her book with a call to the women of Israel to take advantage of their new opportunities, for, in her words, they were now "free not only to believe and obey, but to study and speak of their glorious faith." Anticipating some aspects of twentieth-century feminist analysis, she even recognized that the gendered division of labor in nineteenth-century Western societies provided women with advantages not enjoyed by their husbands and brothers: "it is fully in [women's] power so to do . . . yet more so than men; for the ordinances and commands of our holy faith interfere much less with woman's retired path of domestic pursuits and pleasures than with the more public and more ambitious career of man."[52]

By the end of the nineteenth century and the beginning

50. Ibid., p. 335.
51. Ibid., pp. 9, 13, 317, 325.
52. Ibid., p. 326.

of the twentieth, acculturated middle- and upper-class Jewish women living in Western societies had taken to heart the message of women's potential for religious and social influence in both the domestic and the public sphere, as the image of the "New Woman" expanded the legitimate field of female activity. The writers and the editor of the *American Jewess*, for example, often referred to women as "queens of the home," who were meant to bring about the "reign of religion" and "reinstate the Sabbath to its old glory."[53] At the same time, Rosa Sonneschein, the editor of the magazine, called for women to serve as synagogue trustees and members of Sabbath School boards.[54] In England Lily Montagu, daughter of a prominent Orthodox family, became a central figure in the movement of Liberal Judaism, convinced that women had a contribution to make as spiritual leaders.[55] Building upon the accomplishments of the earlier female charitable associations and upon female activism within the larger society, Jewish women established important, nationwide organizations in the United States, in Germany, and, on a smaller scale, in England. Jewish women who had been active in secu-

53. *American Jewess* 7, no. 2 (May 1898): 97, as cited in Jenna Weissman Joselit, "The Special Sphere of the Middle-Class American Jewish Woman: The Synagogue Sisterhood, 1890–1940," in *The American Synagogue: A Sanctuary Transformed*, ed. Jack Wertheimer (Cambridge: Cambridge University Press, 1987), p. 207.

54. Selma Berrol, "Class or Ethnicity: The Americanized German Jewish Woman and Her Middle Class Sisters in 1895," *Jewish Social Studies* 47, no. 1 (Winter 1985): 29–30.

55. On Montagu, see Ellen M. Umansky, *Lily H. Montagu and the Advancement of Liberal Judaism: From Vision to Vocation* (Lewiston, N.Y.: Edwin Mellen, 1983), and Lily Montagu, *Lily Montagu: Sermons, Letters, Addresses and Prayers*, ed. Ellen M. Umansky (Lewiston, N.Y.: Edwin Mellen, 1985).

lar women's clubs founded the National Council of Jewish Women in Chicago at the time of the World's Fair in 1893. With a membership of almost 50,000 by 1920, it carried out social welfare work and educational programs. It provided well-organized assistance and models of middle-class behavior for needy east European Jewish immigrants and spearheaded the fight against Jewish involvement in the international traffic in prostitution. For the spiritual and cultural growth of its own members, it promoted self-education in Judaism.[56]

The National Council of Jewish Women gave female Jewish leaders the opportunity to present their views of women's role within Judaism. Speaking on "Woman in the Synagogue" at the 1893 Jewish Women's Congress, which gave birth to the council, Ray Frank, a woman who had served as a lay preacher in the frontier conditions of the American West, demonstrated how Jewish women could utilize the doctrine of "true womanhood" to enhance their own status and self-esteem, even while it constrained their aspirations.[57] Frank accepted as self-evident the idea that women were naturally more spiritual than men and that "religion [was] impossible

56. On the National Council of Jewish Women, see Rogow, Gone to Another Meeting, and Sue Levi Elwell, "The Founding and Early Programs of the National Council of Jewish Women: Study and Practice as Jewish Women's Religious Expression" (Ph.D. diss., Indiana University, 1982). For membership figures, see Rogow, Gone to Another Meeting, p. 241. On women volunteer activists in the American Jewish community in the late nineteenth and early twentieth centuries, see June Sochen, Consecrate Every Day: The Public Lives of Jewish American Women, 1880–1980 (Albany: State University of New York Press, 1981), pp. 45–71. On Jews and the fight against prostitution, see Edward Bristow, Prostitution and Prejudice: The Jewish Fight against White Slavery, 1870–1939 (New York: Schocken Books, 1983).

57. Ray Frank, "Woman in the Synagogue," reprinted in Umansky and Ashton, eds., Four Centuries of Jewish Women's Spirituality, pp. 130–36.

without woman."[58] Surveying the important role of women in the survival of the Jews from biblical days to her own time, she defended Judaism's treatment of women and its recognition of mothers as teachers. "When the Lord said to Moses, 'And ye shall be unto Me a nation of priests and a holy nation,'" she asserted, "the message was not to one sex."[59] Indeed, Frank concluded her historical survey with the confident claim that she had proved that women were intellectually equal to men in religious matters and their superiors when it came to practicality. Yet Frank took the opportunity of her address to chastise Jewish women of her own time for failing to prevent the contemporary decline in religious practice and to call upon them to strengthen Judaism from their domestic throne:

> [T]o be identical with man is not the ideal of womanhood. Some things and privileges belong to him by nature; to these, true woman does not aspire; but every woman should aspire to make of her home a temple, of herself a high priestess, of her children disciples, then will she best occupy the pulpit, and her work run parallel with man's. She may be ordained rabbi or be the president of a congregation—she is entirely able to fill both offices—but her noblest work will be at home, her highest ideal, a home. . . . Nothing can replace the duty of the mother in the home. *Nothing can replace the reverence of children, and the children are yours to do as ye will with them.* . . . Mothers, ye can restore Israel's glory, can fulfil the prophecy by bringing the man-child, strong love of the Eternal, to his Maker.[60]

Frank's address reflects the profound internalization of prevailing gender norms even by a woman who flouted those

58. Ibid., p. 130.
59. Ibid., p. 131.
60. Ibid., pp. 135–36. Emphasis in the original.

norms by talking from a public, rather than a domestic, pulpit. Similarly, in welcoming women in 1896 to the first convention of the National Council of Jewish Women, Rebekah Kohut, lecturer, writer, and teacher, hailed Jewish mothers' potential as "saviors of our people." "Every true Jewess is a priestess. . . . If not from our ranks, then from where shall come those who shall teach our children by religious example, and kindle within them the sparks of faith, that which will keep . . . ever glowing the coals of confidence in the God of Israel?"[61] Only occasionally did a communal representative dissent from the exclusive emphasis on the maternal religious role. In a speech delivered at the 1893 Jewish Women's Congress where Ray Frank had spoken, Mary Cohen, a poet, teacher, and communal activist in Philadelphia, praised the inextricable linkage of home and synagogue within Judaism and the importance of domestic ritual, including the preparation of special holiday foods. Cohen's emphasis on the importance of "kitchen Judaism" necessarily highlighted the woman's role. "I can never see, in the sometimes punctilious care with which some Hebrew women prepare their homes for the religious festivals, the ground for annoyance or ridicule which it seems to furnish to many critics," she admitted. But she also referred to the shared responsibility of Jewish parents, rather than of mothers alone: "the synagogue is the home, and the home the synagogue. I mean that the intelligent and devout Hebrew parent is the priest or priestess of the family altar."[62]

American Jewish women were not alone in organizing for

61. Rebekah Kohut, "Welcoming Address, First Convention of the National Council of Jewish Women," in ibid., p. 141.

62. Mary M. Cohen, "The Influence of the Jewish Religion in the Home," in ibid., pp. 137, 136.

philanthropic, educational, and communal political purposes. In Germany in 1904 Jewish women established the Jüdischer Frauenbund, which attained a membership of 35,000 within a decade and 50,000 by the end of the 1920s.[63] The smaller Union of Jewish Women emerged in Great Britain in 1902.[64] The American, British, and German Jewish women's organizations cooperated in the international campaign against white slavery and lobbied for greater recognition for women within their respective Jewish communities. Despite differences in their specific programs stemming from the nature of their home countries and of their respective Jewish communities, all three of these women's organizations asserted a distinct role for women as sustainers of Jewish communal life and guardians against defection from Judaism. Without challenging the primacy of home and domestic responsibilities as the proper focus of women's lives, they reconfigured the boundaries between the domestic and public spheres, although some of their spokeswomen might have been reluctant to acknowledge this. In teaching administrative skills and conferring public positions of authority and responsibility upon their members, they also expanded the range of appropriate female behavior.

In addition to taking upon themselves extensive responsibility for philanthropy and social welfare as part of the middle-class woman's religious and moral burden, American Jewish women in the twentieth century carried their domestic talents into the synagogue and sacralized the home as the site of Jewish observance. It became their mission to make the synagogue more "homey" and to realize the potential of the home

63. Kaplan, *The Jewish Feminist Movement in Germany*, pp. 10–11.
64. Kuzmack, *Woman's Cause*, pp. 49–50, 82–83, 165–68.

as a sacred sphere for the transmission of Judaism. The synagogue sisterhood conceived as a charitable organization—a synagogue-based Ladies' Benevolent Society—declined at the turn of the century as philanthropy became professionalized and centralized. Jewish women then turned their attention to the domestic management of the synagogue. National organizations of synagogue sisterhoods, divided denominationally, gave women a visible role within the synagogue. Most sisterhood members devoted themselves to decorating the sanctuary for festivals, serving tea at the Oneg Shabbat, and promoting attendance at synagogue services. Sisterhoods organized sisterhood Sabbaths (special Sabbath services that honored women), performed manifold housekeeping functions within the synagogue, and took a particular interest in the smooth functioning of the religious schools. Some historians have shown that the Reform sisterhood organization provided a platform for the articulation of demands for greater public participation of women in the synagogue.[65] Reform sisterhoods, for example, often assumed responsibility for conducting services during the slow summer months. In 1924 the president of the Reform National Federation of Temple Sisterhoods could declare:

> Woman has at last found her niche in religious life as well as in civic and political work. We do not find her today relegated to

65. On synagogue sisterhoods, see Joselit, "Special Sphere," pp. 206–30. On women in Orthodox synagogues, see her New York's Jewish Jews, pp. 97–122. For the role of sisterhoods as sources of promotion of equality for women within the synagogue, see Pamela Nadell, "The Beginnings of the Religious Emancipation of American Jewish Women" (paper delivered at the Berkshire Conference of Women Historians, New Brunswick, N.J., 8 June 1990).

the gallery of the synagogue docilely watching the men of the congregation. Her voice is heard on the Temple Board, her advice is asked in the direction of affairs of the Sabbath School, she is in fact a force in the religious community.[66]

On the occasion of the twenty-fifth anniversary of the organization in 1938, its founding president, Carrie Simon, even called for the ordination of women as rabbis.[67]

In the 1920s sisterhood organizations also elaborated upon the stereotypical representation of the woman's domestic role as priestess. The Conservative movement's Women's League, more concerned with Judaizing the home under female auspices than with feminizing the synagogue, sponsored a number of publications designed to facilitate the Jewish housewife's ritual task as she enhanced the Jewishness of her home. Most popular was Deborah Melamed's *The Three Pillars*, first published in 1927. It outlined the obligations of the Jewish woman in the areas of Sabbath and holiday observance, prayer, and child rearing. *The Three Pillars* crystallized the by now familiar view of the woman as the religious and moral arbiter of the Jewish family par excellence and called for the education of women to prepare them for their maternal responsibilities. As Melamed wrote, "The importance of the woman in Jewish life cannot be overestimated, and an intelligent Jewish woman bespeaks a certain amount of Jewish training and education." In describing the Sabbath, she added that "in many homes it is [the Jewish woman] who must assume almost the entire responsibility of fostering her children's religious life and of transmitting to them that spiritual heritage which has moulded her own." By encouraging the observance of *kashrut*,

66. Joselit, *New York's Jewish Jews*, pp. 98–99.
67. Nadell, "Religious Emancipation," p. 11.

the Jewish mother attained two goals: "character building" and inculcating the sense of belonging to "a special people."[68] To facilitate their members' fulfillment of their central role in preserving and transmitting Judaism, in 1931 the Women's League spurred the establishment of a Women's Institute of Jewish Studies by the Jewish Theological Seminary. Reform and Orthodox sisterhood groups, too, took steps to deepen the Jewish knowledge of their members to strengthen ritual observance in the home and to prepare mothers for instilling a positive Jewish identity in their children.[69] The Western, middle-class definition of womanhood thus provided Jewish women with a conservative role but also allowed innovation in expanded educational opportunities for females and a more visible presence in the synagogue.

The adoption of Western bourgeois concepts of female religiosity also had negative consequences for the depiction of Jewish women, at least in the Jewish press. The representation of women and assimilation in public Jewish statements of the nineteenth and early twentieth centuries diverges markedly from the demonstrable historical record, in part due to the failure to recognize the gender differences in both the timing and the extent of Jewish assimilation in nineteenth-century western and central Europe and America. Exploring the contradiction between female experience and female representation uncovers a fundamental ambivalence about the

68. Deborah Melamed, *The Three Pillars: Thought, Worship and Practice for the Jewish Woman* (New York: Women's League of the United Synagogue of America, 1927), pp. 36, 68–69, 41–42. The book was reprinted many times.

69. Nadell, "Religious Emancipation," p. 15; Joselit, *New York's Jewish Jews*, pp. 108–9.

project of assimilation even among male communal leaders who generally supported it.

In the second half of the nineteenth century, as assimilation was proceeding apace in the cities of Europe and the United States, articles critical of Jewish women began to appear regularly in the Jewish press in Germany, France, England, and the United States. Rather than noting the gender differences in Jewish practice which we have documented and chastising men for their defection from the Jewish community, these articles blamed women, particularly mothers, for the signs of radical assimilation that were capturing the attention of Jewish critics. Certainly, this criticism is not wholly surprising, for, as we have seen, bourgeois ideology conferred on wives and mothers responsibility for the moral and religious tone of the home, and Jewish spokesmen had adopted this ideology.[70] If the family was no longer succeeding in transmitting Jewish knowledge and loyalty to the younger generation, then the guardians of the hearth had failed in their task. In preparing their sons so well to enter into the institutions of the larger society, mothers were neglecting the inculcation of a Jewish identity. As the *Archives israélites* noted with regret in 1889, the Jewish woman was not the model of piety she had been only fifty years before: "All the general qualities of the modern woman have developed in her at the expense of the particular qualities of the Jew." And, therefore, "she leaves her children, unfortunately, in absolute ignorance of their faith."[71]

70. See my "The Modern Jewish Family: Image and Reality," in *The Jewish Family: Metaphor and Memory*, ed. David Kraemer (New York: Oxford University Press, 1989), pp. 179–93.
71. *Archives israélites* 50 (1889): 399–400.

This communal expression of disappointment at the failure of Jewish mothers was by no means limited to the French milieu but was articulated in all the societies which had experienced emancipation and assimilation, irrespective of the levels of social and political antisemitism. In 1875 the London *Jewish Chronicle* commented, "[P]ossibly there is no feature of the age more dangerous or more distressing than the growing irreligion of women."[72] Similarly, German Jewish spokesmen took women to task for failing in their sacred responsibility. "Women are giants who carry the world on their shoulders by caring for the home," editorialized one paper. "If the religious home falls, so does the world of religion."[73] In commenting in an 1871 article on the historic piety of Jewish women and the inspiration they offered to their families and communities, Rabbi Kaufmann Kohler lamented the neglect by contemporary Jewish women of their time-honored noble task of bringing spirituality to their homes, and this at a time when Reform had granted them a larger role within the synagogue.[74] And in Texas, too, in the late 1870s Jewish women were pointedly reminded of their responsibilities: "You as daughters of Sarah and Rebecca ought never to forget that it is your sacred duty . . . to instruct your children, to give them a religious and moral training. . . . [R]emember that there is a great debt of responsibility resting upon you, and that you are held accountable for the acts of your children."[75] Some women also

72. *Jewish Chronicle*, 12 Mar. 1875, p. 801.

73. As cited in Kaplan, "Priestess and Hausfrau," p. 62.

74. Goldman, "The Ambivalence of Reform Judaism," pp. 481–82. Kohler continued for decades to voice his disappointment that women had not reinvigorated either the Jewish home or the synagogue. See pp. 490–91.

75. As cited in Wenger, "The Southern Lady and the Jewish Woman."

participated in the critique of Jewish mothers of their time. In her speech at the 1893 Jewish Women's Congress, Ray Frank, for example, castigated her peers:

> Go to the synagogue on Friday night; where are the people? Our men cannot attend, keen business competition will not permit them. Where are our women? Keener indulgence in pleasures will not permit them. . . . With whom lies the blame? Where are the wise mothers of Israel today? . . . That we are now in the position of backsliders is owing to us women.[76]

Fathers are absent from communal discussions about the younger generation, although as lay and rabbinic leaders of the Jewish community they continued to invest time and resources in educational institutions dedicated to the transmission of Jewish culture and identity. In my survey of the nineteenth-century Jewish press of England, France, Germany, and the United States and of public Jewish pronouncements, I have found no references specifically to fathers' responsibilities for the education of their children or for the inculcation of a Jewish identity nor blame of fathers for the defection of their children from the Jewish community. In the gendered project of assimilation the female sex was at the center.

Yet within the preemancipation Jewish community the obligation to educate children, primarily sons, rested precisely upon fathers. In practice the father's obligation was socialized, for the male heads of household within a community assumed responsibility for establishing educational institutions for all the children of the community. Indeed universal literacy in Hebrew and familiarity with the biblical text

---

76. Frank, "Woman in the Synagogue," p. 135.

were communal ideals for all males, and many communities provided basic instruction in reading for girls as well. The transfer of the obligation to educate Jewish youth from fathers and communal institutions to mothers, with reduced supplementary assistance from communal institutions, was, as I have suggested, a major aspect of the assimilation of Western Jewry to the norms of the larger society. It permitted Jewish men to pursue success in the worlds of commerce and civic affairs and to assume leadership positions within the Jewish community while relegating the transmission of Jewish knowledge and identity to the domestic sphere and to women, who, incidentally, had fewer educational and material resources to accomplish the task. By focusing, in the case of Jewish communal critics, on the failure of Jewish women to fulfill their assigned role or, in the case of Freud and other Jewish men who had become highly secularized, on women's eagerness to fulfill it all too well, Jewish men were able to ignore problematic elements within the project of assimilation itself, particularly as they related to their own behavior.

The project of assimilation contained an unacknowledged source of tension: the assumption that limits could be set to assimilation, that Jews would not disappear completely within the larger society, that individual mobility would not conflict with group survival. As the Jewish elite pressed for social and civic equality, their behavior belied that assumption. With each succeeding generation, Jewish learning and practice declined and signs of radical assimilation increased. Men predominated among those who converted and intermarried. Because the bourgeois ideal of female behavior restricted women's access to the public arena and saw religiosity as a feminine attribute, assimilating Jewish women apparently retained more signs of Jewish identification than did the men in their families. The male leadership of the Jewish community would not renounce the social, economic, and psychological benefits of emancipation and adoption of Western culture nor could it devise an effective strategy for promoting Jewish communal persistence without setting limits to individual male ambition. Blaming Jewish mothers for the decline in Jewish knowledge and religious practice enabled Jewish men in western and central Europe to continue the process, and the project, of Jewish assimilation.

The Jews of the West were the first to confront the new political and social conditions that accompanied modernity, but they constituted only a small minority of world Jewry. The much larger Jewish population of eastern Europe was also compelled to redefine its identity and relationship to the larger society. The particular social, political, and cultural contexts of eastern Europe took the process and project of Jewish assimilation, and the gender relations encoded within both, in vastly different directions from the nineteenth-century Western model.

# 2

# Seductive Secularization

In 1913 a Jewish girls' school in Vilna called Yehudiyah, which provided supplementary education for girls aged seven to eighteen, published a publicity pamphlet in Yiddish that lamented the alienation of young Jewish women from Jewish culture and from the Jewish people. According to the anonymous author:

> Once the Jewish daughter ceaselessly absorbed [Jewish] culture from the day of her birth. She was taught no Torah, but the spirit of the Torah already soared over her cradle. In our times, a girl receives no knowledge at all of *Yiddishkayt* [Jewishness]. The first song that she hears is not a Jewish one; the first letter she learns is not from "alef-beis"; the first little story she reads is of foreign life in a foreign tongue. . . . Years go by. The girl becomes ever more distanced from her people, from its culture, from its traditions, from its pride in its past, from its concerns in the present, from its hopes for the future. . . . And this is the result of such an education: the mediocre woman either heads toward apostasy . . . or she arranges her house in a non-Jewish way and yearns her whole life after foreign peoples.[1]

This is a surprising statement to find in one of the most important centers of traditional Jewish life on the eve of the First World War. What does such a text represent? Were the Jews of Poland and Lithuania simply following the assimilatory path blazed by their central European kin some two or three generations earlier? Or was the author of this pamphlet

1. *Froyen-shul "Yehudiyah" in Vilna* (Vilna: B. Kletzkin, 1913), pp. 1–4.

indulging in the pessimistic discourse that has led critics of Jewish communities in all ages to portray their contemporaries as deviants from a glorious past characterized by learning and righteous behavior? What social phenomena were the pamphlet and the school it promoted attempting to address?

By the first decade of the twentieth century most east European Jews realized that their traditional culture was undergoing a process of transformation. Concentrated above all in the Russian Pale of Settlement, they constituted the largest Jewish population of the world. A combination of industrial development and restrictive governmental policy was undermining the economic foundations of Russian Jewry. The building of railroads, the freeing of the serfs, and the new entrepreneurship displayed by the nobility had significantly diminished the Jews' role as middlemen between the rural and urban markets. Moreover, the government sought to exclude Jews from key sectors of the economy.[2] In an effort to assimilate Jews into Russian society and erode their traditional culture, the government had established schools for Jewish children, training more than two generations of a Russified elite. General governmental schools also accepted Jews. The Jewish Haskalah (Enlightenment) movement in Russia had disseminated its rationalist message of self-improvement and called upon Jews to be open to secular European culture. Looking to the West, maskilim (adherents of the Haskalah) held fast to the vision of emancipation and social integration

2. Simon Kuznets, "Immigration of Russian Jews to the United States: Background and Structure," *Perspectives in American History* 9 (1975): 35–124, esp. 53–79; Arcadius Kahan, "The Impact of Industrialization in Tsarist Russia on the Socioeconomic Conditions of the Jewish Population," in *Essays in Jewish Social and Economic History*, ed. Roger Weiss (Chicago: University of Chicago Press, 1986), pp. 1–69.

proclaimed and at least partially realized in France, Germany, and the Austro-Hungarian Empire. An increasingly urbanized Jewish population read the newspapers and books that promoted a secular consciousness. Although the vast majority of Jews in eastern Europe remained traditionally educated and religiously observant, an articulate lay leadership competed with the rabbinic elite and their allies and offered a variety of secular Jewish strategies to fashion Jewish life and identity in the modern world.[3]

A multiplicity of forms of Jewish self-definition and self-expression coexisted among the large Jewish populations of the Russian Empire, Romania, and parts of the Austro-Hungarian Empire. Regional variations were enormous, but it was clear that the traditional Jewish populations of eastern Europe were experiencing the beginnings of a process of assimilation. The socioeconomic, political, and cultural contexts of their assimilation, however, differed dramatically from those of Western Jews. The roles and representation of women diverged accordingly from the Western model.

In the Russian Empire of the late nineteenth century the process of assimilation can best be characterized as a secularization that avoided both denationalization and religious reform. Traditional Jewish practice and learning declined significantly in the West, but the importance assigned religious sentiment in the dominant bourgeois cultures of Western

3. On the development of Russian Jewry in the nineteenth century, see Michael Stanislawski, *Tsar Nicholas I and the Jews* (Philadelphia: Jewish Publication Society, 1983), and Eli Lederhendler, *The Road to Modern Jewish Politics* (New York: Oxford University Press, 1989). On the Haskalah movement, see Steven Zipperstein, *The Jews of Odessa* (Stanford: Stanford University Press, 1985), and Michael Stanislawski, *For Whom Do I Toil?* (New York: Oxford University Press, 1988).

societies encouraged the fashioning of modern versions of Judaism that officially submerged Jewish ethnicity. In fact, in postemancipation Western communities Jews defined themselves as members of a religious minority, even those who no longer observed most Jewish ritual. There was no similar pressure in eastern Europe for Jews to reform their religion and assert an identity based upon it alone. Instead, Jews who broke with traditional Judaism tended to define themselves in terms of ethnicity (except for those politically radical Jews who divested themselves of ethnicity in the name of universalism). The Russian Empire was multiethnic, and Jews were thus not alone in basing their identity on such ethnic characteristics as shared language, culture, and history. The modernizing sectors of Russian society were themselves secularized, most Jews had no hope of rapidly achieving middle-class status like their kin to the west, and the ideologies that spoke to youth who had abandoned traditional religion, whether Jews or Gentiles, were political. Moreover, it was simpler for Jews who sought acculturation and integration to abandon Jewish observance than to institute religious reform. These modernizing Jews confronted far more opposition than in the West, for the institutions and leadership of traditional Judaism continued to dominate the east European kehillah (community), remaining responsible for Jewish education and mobilizing the support of large numbers of Jews. As the stories of Sholom Aleichem reveal so poignantly, Jewish society in Russia was fractured along generational, class, and cultural lines.[4]

Some Jewish women found secular culture and politics particularly attractive because they chafed under the gender

4. In English, see, for example, Selected Stories of Sholom Aleichem (New York: Random House, Modern Library, 1956).

divisions and the consequent educational restrictions of traditional Jewish society. According to *halakha* (Jewish law), women were exempt from the study of Torah, that is, the texts of the Hebrew Bible and of rabbinic learning, whose mastery conferred status upon Jewish men. In practice this exemption became social exclusion. Traditional east European Jews continued to provide a classical Torah education for their sons in *khadorim* (traditional Jewish primary schools; singular, *kheyder*) and *yeshivas* (schools of advanced Talmud study; singular, *yeshivah*), although with increasing frequency Orthodox parents chose to enroll their sons in modern Jewish private schools. In 1898–99, for example, almost 54 percent of Jewish boys still attended *khadorim*.[5] However, the same families that chose for their sons various forms of private Jewish education, whether of traditional or modernized curriculum, often sent their daughters to public primary schools, where they were introduced to secular culture. In Galicia in 1890, for example, the historian Shaul Stampfer has estimated on the basis of governmental statistics that about 40 percent of Jewish girls were enrolled in public primary schools, but only about one quarter of Jewish boys. There is also evidence that families of means hired private tutors to provide their daughters a general education. Most of these parents paid little attention to their daughters' formal Jewish education beyond elementary instruction in reading Yiddish and sufficient Hebrew to follow prayers in the *siddur*. To be sure, as Stampfer has pointed out, women in traditional east European Jewish society were neither ignorant nor illiterate. Even when they had no secular education, most could read Yiddish, and there is considerable evidence that they were avid readers of secular Yiddish litera-

5. Zipperstein, *Jews of Odessa*, p. 130.

ture and of aggadic, ethical, and even mystical religious texts in Yiddish. Two differences between male and female education, however, are significant: (1) boys studied longer than girls and studied texts that were considered more important within the context of Jewish tradition than books women read, and their study was highly valued while female learning was dismissed; (2) when girls were exposed to general education, they experienced a greater disparity between the secular culture available to them and the informal Jewish curriculum they encountered.[6]

Rarely did religiously observant parents include significant formal Jewish learning in their daughters' curriculum. An exception was Rabbi Yehiel Pines, member of a prosperous family renowned for its rabbinic lineage as well as its wealth. In the 1870s and 1880s he supplemented his daughters' attendance at a kheyder for girls in their hometown of Roszinoy by reviewing the material with them at home in the evening and hiring a tutor for them in ḥumash (Bible) and Yiddish writing. This tutoring continued while the girls attended a non-Jewish private school in Mohilev, where they learned Russian, German, and French as well as a full range of secular subjects. An impetus for providing such an extensive Jewish education for their daughters may have been the fact that the family took pride in its learning and at that time had no surviving sons.[7] Puah Rakowski's father, a traditionally observant Jew, provided a Jewish education for his adolescent daughter in

6. Shaul Stampfer, "Gender Differentiation and Education of the Jewish Woman in Nineteenth-Century Eastern Europe," Polin 7 (1992): 63–87. The statistics are on pp. 79–80.

7. Ita Yellin, "Leẓe'eẓ'ai (For my descendants) (Jerusalem: Hamʿarav Printing Press, 1928), pp. 9, 11–12.

Białystok in the late 1870s because she was so enthralled by
Jewish texts and so extraordinarily talented in their study. In
her memoirs Rakowski reported her father commenting ruefully, "It's a shame you were born a girl and not a boy."[8] The
assertion of a fundamental accident of birth was necessary to
rationalize an exception to the rule in the gendered division
of Jewish education.

More common was the experience of Miriam Shor Sperber,
born into a prosperous Hasidic merchant family around 1900.
While her younger brother was instructed in traditional Jewish rabbinic learning by a rabbi from Poland, she and her
older sister were taught only to read Hebrew, which included
study of the *siddur* (prayer book). As she commented in her
memoirs, they learned no laws but absorbed miẓvot (com-
mandments) from the environment. They were taught formu-
las for blessings by their father and mother and their Jewish
cook; they heard Bible stories regularly from their mother on
Sabbath afternoons when she read to them from the *Taytsh
Chumash* (the *Tseneurene*, the compilation of Bible stories and
midrashic commentary for women). They learned the importance of prayer for women from their mother's daily prayer
and learned how a believing Jew behaves in the house, in
business, and in society from their father. Their formal Jewish education, however, paled beside their secular studies.

8. Puah Rakowski, *Zikhroynes fun a yiddisher revolutsionerin* (Memoirs of a
Jewish revolutionary woman) (Buenos Aires: Tsentral-Farband fun Poylishe Yidn in Argentina, 1954), pp. 19 (for the citation) and 20. Ita Kalish,
whose father was a Hasidic rebbe in Otvotsk, reports a similar statement
whispered by her father to himself when she startled her older brother's
Talmud tutor by reciting from memory the *sugyah* (passage) they had been
studying aloud while she sat at the table (Ita Kalish, *Etmolai* [My yesterdays]
[Tel-Aviv: Hakibutz Hameuchad Publishing House, 1970], p. 46).

Studying with a private tutor, a religiously observant woman, they followed a high-school curriculum in literature, history, mathematics, languages, and geography. During the week they read extensively in Russian literature, and on the Sabbath, when Russian books were considered inappropriate to the sanctity of the day, they still read secular works, but in Yiddish. When their father was convinced that they were mature enough, and secure enough in their faith, to have contact with a wider social circle, they attended a Jewish gymnasium (high school) run by Vladimir Jabotinsky's sister and, later, university. Although Miriam Shor Sperber's formal Jewish education was meager and her secular education considerable, she remained faithful to the patterns of traditional Jewish life she experienced in her childhood home.[9] Her example indicates that secular education, which led many Jewish women to break with religious orthodoxy, could also be consonant with traditional religious practice. Still, Sperber's modern higher education would not have equipped her well for marriage to a *yeshivah bokhur* (a *yeshivah* student) with no secular culture.

And Miriam Shor Sperber's experience was atypical. As Puah Rakowski, who devoted her life to Jewish education for girls and to Zionist activism, commented in her memoirs:

> Our people paid dearly [for the traditional view that it was wrong to teach Torah to females]. If our grandfathers and fathers, as spiritual leaders . . . had reversed themselves, so that Torah edu-

9. Miriam Sperber, *Miberdichev ᶜad Yerushalayim: Zikhronot leveit Ruzhin* (From Berdichev to Jerusalem: Recollections of the House of Ruzin) (Jerusalem: privately printed, 1981), pp. 46–48, 51–53. On Jewish women as readers of Yiddish works in the nineteenth century, see David Roskies, "Yiddish Popular Literature and the Female Reader," *Journal of Popular Culture* 10, no. 4 (1977): 852–58.

cation should know no sex difference, so that Jewish daughters, exactly like sons, should be educated in our Torah, in our culture and moral doctrines, who knows how many thousands of Jewish mothers would have been saved from assimilation . . . and thereby also Jewish sons, whom we have lost because of their education, which they received from their assimilated mothers? From our national liberation movement as well we have lost legions of Jewish sons.[10]

Like Rakowski, but years before her memoirs were published, the directors of Vilna's Yehudiyah assailed the common decision of Russian Jews to restrict the formal education of their daughters to secular subjects. Not all Jewish families were as successful as the Shors in providing models of traditional Jewish culture that accommodated secular learning. The spokesmen for Yehudiyah asserted that, in the modern world, living in a Jewish household was not sufficient to guarantee a strong Jewish consciousness for youth whose book learning was limited to European texts taught in a non-Jewish social context. Yehudiyah offered its two hundred students three hours of instruction a day after the conclusion of public school—in Hebrew language, Bible, Mishnah, Midrash, and Jewish history—in order to instill a Jewish nationalist consciousness.[11]

Jewish nationalists were not the only ones to recognize the consequences of ignoring the Jewish education of girls. Beginning in the late eighteenth century in central Europe and continuing into the nineteenth in eastern Europe, maskilim had succeeded in establishing schools for poor girls precisely because their education was of little concern to the Orthodox

10. Rakowski, Zikhroynes, p. 19.
11. Froyen-shul "Yehudiyah" in Vilna, pp. 6, 10, 11, 14.

elite. Schooling for girls under auspices other than the Orthodox community's did not entail bittul Torah (diversion from
Torah study).[12] The Haskalah poet Judah Leib Gordon explicitly used this argument to his own advantage when, in 1866,
he established a girls' academy in Tel'shi in Russian Lithuania. The misguided opposition to modern education on the
part of traditional Jews, he asserted, extended only to boys;
he anticipated no obstacles to providing a modern education
to girls.[13]

By the early years of the twentieth century, even some
Orthodox figures expressed concern about the type of instruction girls received in the traditional community. In 1903,
at a conference of Polish rabbis, Rabbi Menahem Mendel
Lands, a Hasidic leader, criticized the neglect of girls' Jewish education and called for the creation of Orthodox Jewish
schools for girls. His call fell upon deaf ears.[14] About a decade and a half later, however, Sarah Schenirer, a seamstress
and daughter of a Hasidic family, established a study group for
women in Cracow. Eager to spread Torah education among
girls, she secured the support of the Belzer rebbe, a crucial step that provided rabbinical authorization for her radical
idea. In 1918 she opened the first Beys Yaakov school, and
the following year the Orthodox political organization Agudas Yisroel absorbed the school as its educational agency for

12. Rachel Elbaum-Dror, Haḥinukh haʿivri bʾereẓ Yisraʾel (Hebrew education in the land of Israel), vol. 1 (Jerusalem: Yad Yitzhak Ben-Zvi, 1986),
p. 50. Shortly after his arrival in the town of Shavli in Russian Lithuania
in 1860, the Haskalah poet Judah Leib Gordon opened a school for girls
there. Stanislawski, For Whom Do I Toil? pp. 40, 45.

13. Stanislawski, For Whom Do I Toil? p. 77.

14. Deborah Weissman, "Education of Jewish Women," Encyclopedia
Judaica Yearbook, 1986–87, p. 33.

women. From then on Agudas Yisroel promoted Jewish education among women and established Beys Yaakov schools throughout Poland and in Lithuania, Latvia, Czechoslovakia, Romania, Hungary, and Austria. In 1937 there were more than 250 affiliated schools; most of them, like Yehudiyah, were supplementary schools.[15] Similarly, in 1933 the Chofetz Chayim (Rabbi Yisroel Meir Cohen), the leading rabbinic authority in Poland, advocated formal Jewish education for women in response to the conditions of the time, which had undermined religious tradition: "It is surely a great mitzvah to teach girls the Pentateuch and also the other books of Scripture (the Prophets and Writings) and the ethics of the rabbis . . . so that our holy faith will be verified for them. Because if not, the girls are likely to stray completely from the path of the Lord and transgress the foundations of our religion, God forbid."[16]

The common recognition by secular nationalist and Orthodox Jews alike of the deleterious consequences of neglecting girls' Jewish education testifies eloquently to the widespread perception of the problem. In the absence of communal attention, Jewish girls might be lost to the Jewish community.

Although we have evidence of the concern expressed by Jewish leaders, both traditional and modern, about the increasing assimilation of Jewish women, we have little information from women themselves. The "loss of faith" as a prelude to, or concomitant with, the acquisition of secular culture was

15. Deborah Weissman, "Bais Yaakov: A Historical Model for Jewish Feminists," in *The Jewish Woman*, ed. Elizabeth Koltun (New York: Schocken, 1976), pp. 141–43. For a hagiographic essay on Schenirer, see Moshe Prager, "Sarah Schenirer," in *Sefer Krako: ʿIr vʾem beyisraʾel*, ed. Aryeh Bauminger, Meir Bosak, and Natan Gelber (Jerusalem: Mosad Harav Kuk, 1959), pp. 369–76.

16. As cited in Weissman, "Education of Jewish Women," p. 33.

a frequent theme in Hebrew literature of the late-Haskalah and post-Haskalah periods, roughly the last third of the nineteenth century, but that literature was the province of male writers. Jewish women were not part of literary circles of the time. In their autobiographical writings, leading maskilim like Abraham Ber Gottlober and Moses Lilienblum recounted how the stifling education of the kheyder and the yeshivah contributed to the erosion of their faith. In the Haskalah and secular education they found a substitute religion that offered them the possibility of self-transformation and the opportunity to lead their brethren into new paths of redemption. Because of the phenomenon of early marriage for the intellectually precocious adolescent male, women (both wives and mothers-in-law) figured in their stories as obstacles to self-realization and modernization. For young men raised in the traditional Jewish community and yearning to break free, women represented the burden of tradition and the familial obligations that it imposed upon young boys before they had the opportunity to realize their dreams of intellectual growth.[17]

The few women who have described their experiences in memoirs were not literary personalities. They wrote in Yiddish, Hebrew, or English some two generations or more after the appearance of the famous Haskalah autobiographies and recorded the enormous transformations that had occurred in their own lifetimes as a result of secularization and migration.

17. Alan Mintz, Banished from Their Father's Table: Loss of Faith and Hebrew Autobiography (Bloomington: Indiana University Press, 1989); David Biale, "Childhood, Marriage, and the Family in the Eastern European Jewish Enlightenment," in The Jewish Family: Myths and Reality, ed. Steven M. Cohen and Paula E. Hyman (New York: Holmes & Meier, 1986), pp. 45–61; and David Biale, Eros and the Jews: From Biblical Israel to Contemporary America (New York: Basic Books, 1992).

Most seem to have accepted a gradual erosion of traditional Jewish practice as a normal part of relocation to a large city and entry into the work force.

A few offer a different model. At the age of thirteen, while studying with a private tutor, Puah Rakowski was suddenly struck by the awful realization that there may be no God. After wrestling with the idea for six months, she decided that atheism was the right course, and she abandoned the regimen of regular prayer and strict observance that she had followed as a spiritual adolescent living in an Orthodox home.[18]

Ita Kalish, who was born around the turn of the century, also had a radical reaction to her introduction to modernity. She was eager to experience the Torah study that was so important in the court of her Hasidic rebbe father; her father complied with her wishes by providing private tutors. As she wrote in her memoirs, "For many years there was ingrained in my spirit an inferiority complex about being a girl and not a boy. Seeking compensation, I was more diligent in [studying] the five books of Moses in a Yiddish translation that I received as a present from father, and every Sabbath he would quiz me, in happiness and in pride, in the weekly portion."[19] As an adolescent, however, she sought more than traditional learning. She read Moses Mendelssohn's modern Torah commentary, the *biur*, provided to her by her father's private secretary, who admired Mendelssohn's brilliant mind. Studying general subjects with a female tutor, an "assimilated" young woman, she began to read secular books in Yiddish. Her faith was challenged by a Yiddish book about the great pogroms of 1648–49, and she began to ponder whether there was in

18. Rakowski, *Zikhroynes*, pp. 22–23.
19. Kalish, *Etmolai*, p. 46.

fact a reward for following the Torah. Hungry for news of the world outside her father's court, she read Yiddish newspapers in secret, along with her secular books, late at night in feeble light, abetted by a female cousin who slipped them into the house and by a young maid who collaborated in hiding the forbidden reading material. She described her strategy as creating an "underground" in her own home. She also began to steal out to concerts and theatrical performances, entering by way of the back door as the lights were dimming and leaving before the lights were on again.[20]

Kalish's father attributed her desire to abandon the Hasidic way of life to his error in having her instructed in ḥumash at all; in his eyes, this was the beginning of her breaking through the wall of traditionalism. Sensing that she had a "secular soul," he brought her studies with her tutor to an end, much to her distress, and prepared for her shiddikh (arranged marriage).[21] He had expected that his brilliant son-in-law would quickly distract his daughter from her desire for a different kind of life, but he was mistaken, and she continued her secret secularization even after the birth of her daughter. As long as her father was alive, Ita stayed with her husband. Upon her father's death in 1919, however, she left her husband and daughter and, with her two sisters, moved to Warsaw, where their apartment became a center for young lapsed Hasidim.[22]

Kalish felt that daughters of Hasidic families freed themselves more easily from their fathers' authority than did sons.

20. Ibid., pp. 79, 71–74.

21. He claimed she had already learned enough and was ready to get married (ibid., pp. 71, 73, 76).

22. Ibid., pp. 84–85, 91–93, 96. Finding it difficult to attain custody of her daughter, Zina, she kidnapped her and moved to Berlin, from which she emigrated to Palestine in 1933.

They were more likely to have some secular education than were their brothers. She noted with some surprise that in Warsaw there were even Hasidic families that mixed Hasidism with assimilation, in a highly gendered fashion: "The sons went to a *shtibl* [a small synagogue/house of study] and learned *gemora* [Talmud]—and the girls studied in foreign schools and were educated in the purity of Polish culture." Young men from Hasidic families, she felt, were more drawn to the culture they sought to leave than were their sisters; the young men felt as though their *peyis* (sidecurls) were still tucked behind their ears and a Hasidic *niggun* (melody) were humming within them. Even when they broke with the past, they remained foreign to the new world all their lives.[23] Kalish's observations may reflect not only the differences in education between boys and girls in Hasidic families but also the special status that accrued to males, who were privileged to have a more intimate relation with their rebbe than were females. Moreover, the institutional framework of male learning created an intense communal bond among young males, and girls seem to have had no parallel structure that integrated them within a community.

Puah Rakowski and Ita Kalish, the first born in 1865 and the second about 1900, were unusual in the radicalism of their breaks with the traditionalism of their families. The other nineteen memoirs written by east European women born in this period that I have read, though less dramatic in their narratives, suggest the range of educational possibilities available to Jewish women in eastern Europe.[24] Although parents in

23. Ibid., pp. 99–101. The quotation is from p. 101.
24. The additional memoirs are Ita (Pines) Yellin, *Leze'eza'ai*; Bas Yonah [Sheyndl Dvorin], *Em labanim (Zikhronotai)* (A mother of children [My memo-

learned and wealthy families generally provided some Jewish education for their daughters, ranging from study in a *kheyder* to private tutoring, it was always less substantial than their brothers' and than the secular instruction they received in a public school, in a private Jewish school, or through private tutors. In several cases mothers or grandmothers, per-

ries]) (Pinsk: Druk Dolinko, 1935); Shoshana Lishensky, *Miẓror zikhronotai* (From the bouquet of my memories) (Jerusalem: Dfus Merkaz, 1942); Hinda [Rosenblatt] Bergner, *In di lange vinternekht: Mishpokhe zikhroynes fun a shtetl in Galizie, 1870–1900* (In the long winter nights: Family memories from a shtetl in Galicia, 1870–1900) (Montreal: privately published, 1946); Bella Chagall, *Burning Lights* (1946; reprint, New York: Schocken Press, 1962); Fanny Edelman, *Der shpigel fun leben* (The mirror of my life) (New York: Shulsinger Brothers Printers, 1948); Rokhl Kositza, *Zikhroynes fun a bialystoker froy* (Memoirs of a woman from Białystok) (Los Angeles: Schwartz Printing Co., 1964); Zelda Edelstein, *Bdarkhei avot* (In the ways of the fathers) (Jerusalem: privately printed, 1970); Sheyna Korngold, *Zikhroynes* (Memoirs) (Tel Aviv: Farlag Idpress, 1970); Bilhah Dinur, *Lenechdotai: Zikhronot mishpaḥah vesipurei ḥavayot* (For my granddaughters: Family memories and stories of experiences), arranged and edited by Ben Zion Dinur (Jerusalem: privately printed, 1972); Bella Fogelman, *Mibeit aba ʿad halom* (From my father's house to here) (Kiryat Motzkin: privately printed, 1974); Esther Rosenthal-Shnaiderman, *Oyf vegn un umvegn: Zikhroynes, gesheʿeneshn, perzenlekhkeytn* [Of roads and detours: Memories, events, personalities], 3 vols. (Tel Aviv: Farlag "Hamenora," 1974); Haya Kirshenbaum, *Zikhronot meʿir huladti, Meliẓ* (Memories from the city of my birth, Melitz) (n.p., n.d.; published by family after the author's death in 1976); Frances Senior Melamed, *Janova* (Cincinnati: Janova Press, 1976); Sperber, *Miberdichev ʿad Yerushalayim*; Rivka Guber, *Morasha lehanḥil* (A legacy to pass on) (Jerusalem: Kiryat Sefer, 1981); Zehava Berman, *Bedarki sheli* (In my own way) (Jerusalem: Elyashar, 1982); Malka Heinman, *Zikhronot shel Malka* (Memoirs of Malka) (Jerusalem: privately printed, 1983); Tova Berlin-Papish, *Ẓelilim shelo nishkḥu: Mimohilev ʿad Yerushalayim* (Sounds that were not forgotten: From Mohilev to Jerusalem) (Tel Aviv: Reshafim, 1988). On women's biographies and memoirs, see Carolyn G. Heilbrun, *Writing a Woman's Life* (New York: Norton, 1988).

haps compensating for their own missed opportunities for education, made sure that their daughters or granddaughters received the instruction that they sought. Shoshana Lishensky's mother and grandmother favored sending her and her sister to learn Russian with a tutor who had been brought to their town to teach the Jewish boys (so that they would be able to get along if drafted into the army), but her grandfather, a rabbi, was opposed. Her grandmother also secretly funded their membership in the local lending library. Bilhah Dinur relates, too, that her mother supported her desire to study in a gymnasium, while her father opposed it, in part because it would expose her to a foreign world she might seek to enter.[25]

The gendered division of education among east European Jews was not the only factor facilitating the secularization of Jewish girls and women. The middle-class cult of domesticity that prevailed among Jews in Western countries by the second half of the nineteenth century did not penetrate deeply into the lives of Russian Jews. To be sure, the maskilim, who promoted modern education for Jewish children of both sexes, presumed that girls educated in the spirit of the Haskalah would acquire all of the qualities of the European bourgeois woman. They would be graced by their knowledge of French, music, calligraphy, needlepoint, and etiquette, in addition to Russian, Hebrew, and Bible.[26] However, the vast majority of Jewish women in nineteenth- and early-twentieth-century eastern Europe grew to maturity in a society that did not facili-

25. Lishensky, Miẓror zikhronotai, pp. 21, 23; Dinur, Lenechdotai, p. 32. Lishensky's older sister had briefly studied at a gymnasium without her grandfather's knowledge, though they lived with him, but she had to withdraw when he found out. She had changed into her school uniform at a friend's house (p. 25).

26. Stanislawski, For Whom Do I Toil?, pp. 45, 77, 86.

tate the division between the public and domestic realms that was essential for the emergence of the middle-class lady.

Jewish women, of necessity, participated actively in secular public economic life. Although they were excluded from voting or assuming positions of leadership within the *kehillah* and from public roles within the synagogue, they assumed responsibility for contributing to the support of their households.[27] There also existed an elite of learned families that realized the Ashkenazi cultural ideal of full-time Torah study for men, a situation which imposed upon wives the primary obligation for sustaining the family economically.[28] The overwhelming majority of east European Jewish males had neither the talent, the education, nor the resources to become Torah scholars. They worked as merchants or artisans. The existence of the cultural ideal of male learning and female labor, however, legitimated the presence of women in the world of commerce and artisanry as well as their cultivation of character traits that would ensure the survival of the family. Memoirs of east European Jews describing their childhoods from the last third of the nineteenth century through the First World War are replete with references to mothers whose work as seamstresses, storekeepers, peddlers, or even sellers of whiskey to the local peasants kept food on their families' tables.[29]

27. On the "paradoxical place" of women in east European Jewish society, see Susan Glenn, *Daughters of the Shtetl: Life and Labor in the Immigrant Generation* (Ithaca: Cornell University Press, 1990), pp. 8–49.

28. For the stresses on family life that resulted, see Immanuel Etkes, "Marriage and Torah Study among the *Lomdim* in Lithuania in the Nineteenth Century," in *The Jewish Family: Metaphor and Memory*, ed. David Kraemer (New York: Oxford University Press, 1989), pp. 153–78.

29. On whiskey selling, see Joseph Morgenstern, *I Have Considered My Days* (New York: Yiddish Kultur Farband, 1964), p. 14. On meat peddling,

The strong, capable working woman was the dominant cultural ideal, in contrast to the ideal of woman as the creator of a domestic haven (or heaven) that prevailed in the bourgeois West.

As the historian Susan Glenn has pointed out, most Jewish marriages in eastern Europe involved a breadwinning partnership that "gave Jewish wives some family authority, a knowledge of the marketplace, and a certain worldliness."[30] Although the Russian census of 1897 counted only about 22 percent of Jewish women between the ages of fourteen and fifty-nine as economically active—that is, engaged in income-earning labor outside the home—that figure understates women's economic role. Women who assisted their husbands in family businesses or who ran the businesses during their husbands' frequent absences were not counted as workers by the census takers.[31] Wealthy east European Jew-

---

see Rebecca Himber Berg, "Childhood in Lithuania," in *Memoirs of My People*, ed. Leo Schwarz (New York: Schocken, 1963), pp. 271–72. On sewing and sale of goods produced as well as keeping a store for shoemaking tools, see Edelstein, *Bedarkhei avot*, pp. 5, 65. On street peddling, see Chagall, *Burning Lights*, pp. 18–19. On shopkeeping, see Bas Yonah, *Em labanim*, pp. 3–4; Edelman, *Der shpigel fun leben*, p. 12 (Edelman's mother-in-law bore almost complete responsibility for the family store because the customers were Gentiles and her father-in-law spoke no "goyish"); Rose Pesotta, *Days of Our Lives* (New York: Excelsior, 1958), p. 76; Chagall, *Burning Lights*, pp. 25–28, 154, 156; Heinman, *Zikhronot shel Malka*, p. 3; Kalish, *Etmolai*, pp. 40–41. For a widow keeping a milk stand in the marketplace of Yekaterinaslav, see Guber, *Morasha lehanhil*, pp. 33–34. On the wife of a Hasidic rebbe supporting the family as a money changer, see Kalish, *Etmolai*, p. 13.

30. Glenn, *Daughters of the Shtetl*, p. 14.

31. Kahan, "The Impact of Industrialization in Tsarist Russia on the Socioeconomic Conditions of the Jewish Population," pp. 6, 64–65; Glenn, *Daughters of the Shtetl*, pp. 12–16.

ish men may have sought a purely domestic role for their wives, as did their compatriots to the west, but the presence of a large proportion of adult Jewish females in the public economic sphere conferred upon women a measure of independence and a variety of social contacts that were not possible for middle-class women, whose lives were bounded by the social norms of the bourgeois cult of domesticity, which transcended national boundaries.

The maskilim, who promoted the acquisition by Jews of secular education and their acculturation to the norms of educated Russians, expressed ambivalence about women's involvement with work outside the home and attempted to influence Jews to reshape their economic patterns. Although the early maskilim took working wives for granted and praised their contribution to the support of their families, later maskilim sharply criticized the phenomenon of female labor in the marketplace, because they saw it as linked with the traditional ideal of the full-time Torah scholar whose wife assumed the role of family breadwinner. Working women, they argued, abandoned their obligations in the home, where they were responsible for housework and for educating their children. Consequently, their children were more likely to become ill. Women's labor to earn money also demoralized their husbands, who were tempted to be idlers. Moreover, the economic activity of women outside the home was liable to corrupt them morally, because of the possibilities for illicit sex available to women who worked in inns or cafés or as peddlers. As the historian Mordekhai Levin summed up this critique, "The phenomenon of women's commerce leads to commerce in women." Maskilim also believed that strident haggling and the pursuit of material wealth for its own sake degraded women's characters. Finally, the maskilim viewed women's participation in commerce as invariably leading to a decline in the dignity of the Jewish marketplace because women were seen as promoting greater competitiveness and crassness than men.[32]

These criticisms of the working woman depended upon a view of normative gender roles different from the traditional east European Jewish model, which accepted both female physical stamina and female activity in the marketplace. By the last third of the nineteenth century *maskilim* aspired to attain a Jewish version of middle-class domesticity rooted in a definition of women's role that stressed their maternal and homemaking functions and limited them to the home. Because their female ideal was fragile and vulnerable, *maskilim* perceived the skills typical of petty commerce, when practiced by women, as a particular assault on the image of the Jewish community as a whole. Commerce devalued Jewish women and hence contributed to the lack of respect in which all Jews were held. Although some *maskilim* in the second half of the nineteenth century recognized that women working outside the home were more productive than housewives and raising Jewish productivity was one of their central goals,[33] secularly educated male Jewish writers generally thought that women belonged in the home. A 1902 article in a weekly Yiddish newspaper published in Cracow and aimed at women asserted that women who participated in the labor market be-

32. The discussion in this paragraph is based upon Mordekhai Levin, *Erkhei ḥevrah vekalkalah bᵓidiologia shel tekufat hahaskalah* (Social and economic values in the ideology of the Haskalah period) (Jerusalem: Mosad Bialik, 1975), pp. 151–53. The quotation is from p. 153. I would like to thank Richard Menkis for bringing this book to my attention.

33. Ibid., p. 153.

yond the accepted mode of helping out their husbands a bit caused much harm to their husbands and assisted their families not at all. Not only did women's labor drive down wages and thereby increase Jewish poverty, but working women also could not fulfill their valuable tasks of housework and child rearing. No caretaker could replace the mother, who "makes her children better, freer, happier." Moreover, working women brought into their homes the bitter feelings engendered in the workplace.[34] Nevertheless, despite the attempt by maskilim and post-Haskalah intellectuals to transform the contours of work and family for eastern European Jews, economic reality dictated two working parents for most Jews while traditional Jewish society continued to legitimate female support of the Torah scholar's family.

The socioeconomic and cultural contexts in eastern Europe facilitated women's assimilation through their work patterns and access to secular education. Consequently, a greater proportion of Jewish women in eastern Europe took the lead in the process of assimilation than in the countries of western and central Europe and the United States, although the pace and dimensions of assimilation were less extreme. To be sure, even in interwar Poland, which acquired its independence after the First World War, a substantial segment, probably the majority, of Jews remained traditional in their self-consciousness and their religious observance until their murder by the Nazis. The women among the traditionalists, although they modernized their clothing in the interwar years, remained Yiddish-speaking models of religious piety, modest in dress, strongly committed to traditional culture,

34. Di yudishe froyenvelt 14 (1 Oct. 1902): 3.

71

and still involved in commerce.[35] In some wealthy Jewish homes where acculturation occurred relatively early, women replicated the conservative function that seems to have been typical in the West. Pauline Wengeroff gives poignant testimony of this phenomenon. Born in 1833 into a traditionally observant family, she married a Minsk banker and, in the first decade of the new century, wrote her memoirs to lament the ravages of radical assimilation in her own household (among her husband and sons) and to offer a portrait of traditional Jewish life of the past. Although she saw her own experience as female upholder of traditional practice against male assimilatory practices as typical of her circle, she seems to be highly unusual in the context of east European Jewry of her time.[36]

Over the course of several generations, from the second half of the nineteenth century through the interwar years, a significant segment of east European Jewish women secularized and adapted to the culture of their respective social classes. In schematic terms, the women who abandoned tradition in whole or in part went from covering their hair with a scarf

35. Among Jews who fell within the general boundaries of eastern Europe, those of Bohemia, Moravia, and Hungary took the lead in assimilation. See Ezra Mendelsohn, *The Jews of East Central Europe between the World Wars* (Bloomington: Indiana University Press, 1983), pp. 17–22, 87–91, 133–35, 201; Celia S. Heller, *On the Edge of Destruction: Jews of Poland between the Two World Wars* (New York: Columbia University Press, 1977), p. 146. Heller's estimate that the Orthodox-traditionalists composed about one-third of Poland's Jewish population in the 1930s is a low one (p. 144).

36. Pauline Wengeroff, *Memoiren einer Grossmutter: Bilder aus der Kulturgeschichte der Juden Russlands im 19. Jahrhundert* (Berlin: Verlag von M. Poppelauer, 1913). On Wengeroff, see Shulamit Magnus, "Pauline Wengeroff and the Voice of Jewish Modernity," in *Gender and Judaism*, ed. Tamar Rudavsky (New York: New York University Press, forthcoming).

(tikhl) upon marriage to wearing a wig (shaytl) to choosing to display their own hair.[37] Among converts to Christianity, women appear to have taken an increasingly prominent role. In Cracow, the center of Jewish life in Galicia, in the last fourteen years of the nineteenth century women constituted more than two-thirds of the 379 Jewish converts (see table). The conversion records of the Lithuanian consistory of the Russian Orthodox Church covering the years 1819–1911 provide information on 244 Jewish converts and reveal that from the 1860s on, women accounted for the majority of the converts.[38] In the years 1900–1911 they were 65 percent of the converting group. The small number of Jews who converted solely because of religious conviction rather than for pragmatic reasons, such as to advance one's career or, from the opposite end of the social spectrum, to stay out of jail, were all women. Like the men, most of the women converts came from the poorest stratum of Russian Jewry; they were, in the historian Michael Stanislawski's words, "the destitute and the desperate."[39] Since single women were far more numerous than single men among the converts, lower-class women, whose possibilities for marriage in the Jewish community were limited because of their lack of dowries, probably were convert-

37. After Hinda Rosenblatt Bergner (born 1870) was married (through an arranged match) in 1891, she wore a shaytl only once, to her first appearance in the synagogue after her wedding, because her mother pleaded with her to do so. She described how funny she looked with the wig placed upon her own hair. See her In di lange vinternekht, pp. 87–88.

38. Michael Stanislawski, "Jewish Apostasy in Russia: A Tentative Typology," in Jewish Apostasy in the Modern World, pp. 189–205. The statistics on gender appear on p. 200.

39. Ibid., p. 202.

ing to marry Christian men of the same social level whom they had met initially through economic contacts. While recognizing the danger of generalizing from such a small sample of the 69,400 Jews who converted to Russian Orthodoxy during the nineteenth century, Stanislawski suggests tentatively that the disproportionate representation of women among

Jewish Converts in Cracow

| Year | Males | Females | Single | Married | Total |
|---|---|---|---|---|---|
| 1887 | 12 | 16 | 24 | 4 | 28 |
| 1888 | 6 | 20 | 26 | 0 | 26 |
| 1889 | 5 | 18 | 20 | 3 | 23 |
| 1890 | 4 | 22 | 25 | 1 | 26 |
| 1891 | 10 | 16 | 24 | 2 | 26 |
| 1892 | 9 | 21 | 30 | 0 | 30 |
| 1893 | 12 | 18 | 29 | 1 | 30 |
| 1894 | 5 | 15 | 19 | 1 | 20 |
| 1895 | 6 | 13 | 18 | 1 | 19 |
| 1896 | 8 | 17 | 23 | 2 | 25 |
| 1897 | 9 | 29 | 34 | 4 | 38 |
| 1898 | 11 | 19 | 28 | 2 | 30 |
| 1899 | 15 | 15 | 27 | 3 | 30 |
| 1900 | 8 | 20 | 27 | 1 | 28 |
| Total | 120 | 259 | 354 | 25 | 379 |

Source: These statistics are taken from Meir Bosak, "Yehudei Krakov bemaḥaẓit hashniyah shel hameah hatsha-ʿesrei" (The Jews of Cracow in the second half of the nineteenth century), in Sefer Krako, ed. Aryeh Bauminger, Meir Bosak, and Natan Gelber (Jerusalem: Mosad Harav Kuk, 1959), p. 109. I would like to thank Hillel Kieval for bringing this source to my attention.

the Jewish converts in the latter half of the period points to the lesser success of women in accommodating to the "new social, economic, political, and cultural conditions than their brothers, husbands, and sons."[40] These limited conversion records, then, substantiate the assessment of Jewish educators of various ideological perspectives that women were less well prepared for their encounter with Russian culture once the barriers of Jewish segregation were lowered.

Jewish women's vulnerability to the lure of the larger society, whether perceived as Christian or secular, was a product of their social situation. Trained by the gender division of traditional Jewish society to take the initiative, at least economically; respected for their abilities to manage; aware of the value attached to Jewish learning, from which they were largely excluded—Jewish girls often hungered for education and dedicated themselves to acquire it. An observant adolescent like Sheyndl Dvorin learned Hebrew and Bible from her brother-in-law, who was teaching his son, and took her Bible to bed with her, despite her father's displeasure. For years, she frustrated shadkhonim (marriage brokers) as well as her parents by rejecting every potential bridegroom so that she could study in her spare time. Testimony to her successful self-education is the fact that she wrote her memoirs in Hebrew.[41]

More common were young women who lost their faith, had

40. Ibid., p. 200.

41. Bas Yonah, Em labanim, pp. 6–16. Many of the memoir writers resisted initial attempts to arrange marriages for them, thereby delaying their marriages. In no case did they forestall marriage completely. Fanny Edelman chose to emigrate to America at the age of fourteen in part because she wanted to choose her own bridegroom (Der shpigel fun leben, p. 19).

contact with secular culture, and pursued opportunities that they perceived newly open to them. Thus, despite anti-Jewish discrimination, some Jewish women of the middle and upper classes made heroic efforts to acquire secondary education, enrolling in gymnasia or, after the introduction of a strict numerus clausus in 1887, studying privately as externs to take the exams that would prepare them for university courses. Despite the fact that she was married and the mother of two, the twenty-three-year-old Puah Rakowski, for example, managed in 1888 to persuade her husband and parents (who temporarily assumed care of her children) to permit her to study to become a teacher. Her ostensible goal was to enable her to support her family better (her husband had lost her dowry) while her husband devoted much of his time to Torah learning; her real goal, in addition to satisfying her profound thirst for knowledge, was to acquire a profession that would permit her to bring an end to her miserable marriage, arranged when she was sixteen. She succeeded in both her personal quests, becoming the director of a Jewish school for girls in Warsaw, a feminist and Zionist activist, and a successful translator. In her school Rakowski not only provided both Jewish and general education to her students but also instilled in them the recognition that there was more in an adolescent girl's life than waiting for her shiddikh (destined match).[42]

Around 1900 Sheyne Korngold, the older sister of Golda Meir, fought her mother for the right to study instead of being apprenticed as a seamstress. The existence of a school for poor

42. Rakowski, Zikhroynes, pp. 40, 46–54, 64–65; Esther Rosenthal-Shnaiderman describes Rakowski as the founder and director of the first middle school for Jewish girls in Warsaw. See her Oyf vegn un umvegn, p. 290.

Jewish children enabled her to win the battle and, as she later commented in her memoirs, to change her life.[43] Other Jewish women emigrated westward for the express purpose of studying at European universities. At the University of Paris in the decade before the First World War, for example, Russian and Romanian women, most of them Jewish, made up more than one-third of all the female students and about two-thirds of those who were of foreign origin.[44]

In the turbulent world of Russian Jewry at the turn of the twentieth century, women also took advantage of political movements that offered them opportunities for activism and leadership. Like their brothers, young Jewish women who had broken with traditional religion were dazzled by the array of ideological parties that sought to improve the status and condition of the Jews and/or transform Russian society through revolution. Jewish youth who remained socially and emotionally connected to Jews and the Jewish community had a number of choices. They could join the Bund, the Jewish wing of the revolutionary Russian Social Democratic Labor Party, which advocated a socialist revolution and the achievement of national cultural autonomy in Russia for the Yiddish-speaking masses of the working class. They could affiliate with any of the various branches of the Zionist movement, which sought to reestablish the Jews as an independent people in their ancestral homeland. Or they could become adherents of Territorialism, which recognized the Jews as a national entity but rejected the assertion that Palestine was the only,

43. Korngold, *Zikhroynes*, pp. 39–41.

44. Nancy Green, "L'émigration comme émancipation: Les femmes juives d'Europe de l'Est à Paris, 1881–1914," *Pluriel* 27 (1981): 56–58.

or best, territory appropriate for the rescue of Jews through the establishment of a nationalist settlement.[45] Of all these options, politicized Jewish women gravitated disproportionately to the Bund, apparently because it included women in leadership positions.

When the General Jewish Labor Union in Russia and Poland —familiarly known as the Bund—was established in 1897 in a clandestine meeting on the outskirts of Vilna, two women were among the thirteen founding delegates.[46] The historian Henry Tobias's biographical notes of the most-important early Bundists (those active until 1905) include six women among the forty-eight figures listed.[47] J. S. Hertz's biographical collection of Bundist leaders includes 55 profiles of women among its 320 entries.[48] Even more important was the number of women in the middle ranks of leadership as well as among the general membership, where women composed about one-third of the total. Women participated as organizers of workers, writers for the cause, fund-raisers, and speakers in street meetings. They published and distributed illegal literature and served as couriers for political messages, smuggling informa-

45. On the political choices available to Russian Jewish youth and the social determinants of those choices, see Robert Brym, *The Jewish Intelligentsia and Russian Marxism* (New York: Schocken Books, 1978). For a history of the Jewish revolutionary movements in Russia, see Jonathan Frankel, *Prophecy and Politics: Socialism, Nationalism, and the Russian Jews, 1862–1917* (Cambridge: Cambridge University Press, 1981).

46. Henry Tobias, *The Jewish Bund in Russia: From Its Origins to 1905* (Stanford: Stanford University Press, 1972), p. 66.

47. Ibid., pp. 347–53. They are Evgeniia Gurvich, Anna Heller, Tsivia Hurvich, Marya Zhaludsky, Pati Srednitsky, and Rosa Levit.

48. J. S. Hertz, ed., *Doires Bundistn*, 2 vols. (New York: Ferlag Unser Tsait, 1956).

tion hidden in their voluminous skirts. Bilhah Dinur, for example, a young teacher at a girls' vocational school in Dvinsk in 1902, often smuggled material for the Bund. She gave up the activity, however, when she was sent on a mission with a suitcase of weapons and decided that her arrest would endanger her school, to which she was devoted.[49] Women were particularly useful in clandestine activities like smuggling because of the gender assumptions of the day that presumed that women did not have a developed political consciousness. Although gender was never a major analytical category for Bundist intellectuals and activists (they presumed that such tasks as nursing and kitchen chores would be undertaken by women), the movement was committed in theory to equality of the sexes, an equality to be achieved in due course as a consequence of the socialist revolution. That commitment to gender equality was important to women Bundists, who broke with traditional patterns of female life and often with their families. These women radicals sought assurances that they would have a chance to influence the course of history along with their male comrades.[50]

The Zionist movement also recruited young women to its cause. The First Zionist Congress, which took place, like the founding of the Bund, in 1897, included only about a dozen women among its 250 delegates.[51] In Czarist Russia and later in interwar Poland the movement seems to have been less suc-

49. Dinur, Lenechdotai, pp. 42–43.

50. Harriet Davis-Kram, "The Story of the Sisters of the Bund," Contemporary Jewry 5, no. 2 (1980): 27–43.

51. Michael Berkowitz, Zionist Culture and West European Jewry before the First World War (Cambridge: Cambridge University Press, 1993), p. 19. Wives and daughters of delegates also attended the sessions. See David Vital, The Origins of Zionism (Oxford: Oxford University Press, 1975), pp. 356–57.

cessful than the Bund in promoting women to the leadership ranks. Zionist leaders frequently lamented their failure to attract the active support of the masses of Jewish women. Both the reluctance of the Orthodox Mizrachi movement (composed of Orthodox Zionists) to recognize women as potential leaders and the tendency of *ḥalutzim* (male pioneers) in *hakhsharah* (preparation) centers to treat their female coworkers like maids diminished the allure of Zionism for women seeking avenues of political activism.[52] Although in 1902 Puah Rakowski, who was a tireless activist within the ranks of the leftist Poalei-Zion, a major Zionist-socialist party, optimistically reflected that Zionist leaders were increasingly recognizing the importance of involving women in the movement and noted great progress at the Zionist meeting in Minsk, she later expressed disappointment. Looking back on the movement in her memoirs, written toward the end of her long life, she observed: "Jewish daughters from the middle classes had no interest in the concept of national revival. The first bearers of the idea of Hibbat Zion [Love of Zion], the rabbis and simple pious Jews, did not admit women into their circles. . . . The 'Bnai Moshe' [an early elite Zionist group], too, closed its doors to women."[53] The traditionalists' and the intellectual elite's deprecation of women's public role thus deflected talented Jewish women from organized Jewish life into the ranks of secular organizations. Although secular Zionist orga-

52. For discussion of the "woman problem," see Ezra Mendelsohn, *Zionism in Poland: The Formative Years, 1915–1926* (New Haven: Yale University Press, 1981), pp. 339–41.

53. Puah Rakowski, "Di froyen oyf di minsker asefo" (Women at the Minsk meeting), *Di yudishe froyenvelt* 13 (24 Sept. 1902): 1–3; Rakowski, *Zikhroynes*, p. 81.

nizations attempted to present Zionism as a movement for all Jews, they lost momentum to other political groups that more aggressively rejected the gendered division of traditional Jewish society.

Despite the recognized appeal of secular movements to Jewish women and the deleterious effects of inadequate Jewish education, Jewish male leadership in eastern Europe did not give the same attention to women in their published pronouncements as did their counterparts in the West. There were occasional articles in the Hebrew and Yiddish press about the social problem of prostitution[54] or about such exotic figures as a young Jewish female anarchist assassin.[55] Some newspapers also covered general women's issues as a regular part of their journalistic beat. In the first six months of 1913, for example, the Yiddish daily Der fraynd, published in Saint Petersburg, included articles on the women's suffrage movement in England, on women lawyers, on women's voting rights around the world, on women and world peace, and on Jews and the white slave trade.[56] One article pointed out that modern women were dissatisfied with their lot all over the world and, with more and more of them entering the work force, could no longer be thought of only as wives and mothers.[57] Yet, few Jewish journalists focused on Jewish women when they wrote about women's issues.

One weekly newspaper devoted to issues of women and

54. E.g., Ha-Maggid 37, no. 73 (9 Apr. 1897), and Di naye velt (Warsaw) 2, no. 157 (9 July 1910): 3.

55. Di naye velt 2, no. 90 (19 Apr. 1910): 1.

56. Der fraynd 12 (14 Jan. 1913): 2; 21 (24 Jan. 1913): 1; 29 (3 Feb. 1913): 3; 122 (28 May 1913): 3; 143 and 144 (24 and 25 June 1913): 2.

57. Ibid. 41 (17 Feb. 1913): 2.

the family did appear in Cracow for six months in 1902. Entitled Di yudishe froyenvelt (The Jewish women's world), the paper boasted that it was the first Jewish journal to represent the interests of Jewish women. Although its editor and virtually all of its writers were men, it deliberately pointed its text with vowels to make reading easier for its presumably minimally educated female readership.[58] Like most east European turn-of-the-century commentators on Jewish life, the male staff of Di yudishe froyenvelt understood that times had changed and that women had to adapt, if only, as they commented, to answer their children's questions. The paper's purpose, therefore, was instructional—to give women the knowledge they needed and which they could not find in traditional musar (ethical) literature or in Yiddish belles lettres. Defining what women needed to know in the broadest terms, the paper included practical columns on health, child rearing, and housework; "scientific articles on nature and people" that would be "of interest to the Jewish woman as a human being and a mother"; articles on economic issues; fiction and book reviews; biographies of famous women to serve as role models; articles on Jewish history "to inspire love of the Jewish people"; and information on what was happening in the world of women and, more specifically, of Jewish women.[59] The paper also addressed contemporary questions of women's status and manifestations of women's

58. Di yudishe froyenvelt 1 (13 June 1902): 5. The editor was Moses Deutscher. A column on housekeeping seems to have been written by a woman, and articles by women appeared in vols. 9 (27 Aug. 1902) and 13 (24 Sept. 1902). A comment on the vocalization of the text appeared in the first issue.

59. Ibid. 1 (13 June 1902): 2, 4, 5.

desire for equality. Its writers' opinions ranged from those who felt that women had ceased to acknowledge, unlike their mothers and grandmothers, that in their difference from men lay their strength, to those who expressed sympathy for feminism and for women's demands for equal rights.[60] One writer sympathetic to women's desire for equality also pointed, like the Zionist and Orthodox critics cited earlier, to the flaws in the Jewish education of women. Secularly educated Jewish women, he asserted, "go away from us, simply, without elaborate witty explanations [khokhmas] and questions, exactly as though they were throwing away clothes."[61]

After the First World War some Jewish women found in feminism the ideology that best analyzed their own situation and provided a platform for the attainment of economic, social, and political equality. The war disrupted the lives of Polish and Russian Jews and compelled them to pay attention to international politics. Through the Yiddish press Jewish women became increasingly aware of the activities and achievements of feminist movements across Europe. In 1918 Puah Rakowski published a pamphlet, "The Jewish Woman," that combined feminism with Zionism. Asserting the importance of women's activity in a variety of movements for social reform, she lamented the minimal involvement of contemporary women in the Zionist movement. Although Herzl's political Zionism had twenty years before given them voting rights in Zionist elections, women had not taken advantage

60. For an example of the first, see David Frishman, "Di froy (a bisl froyen psikhologia)," in ibid. 2 (8 July 1902): 1–5, and 3 (16 July 1902): 1–5; for an example of the second, see N. Tcherniak, "Froyen egoizm," in ibid. 10 (3 Sept. 1902): 1–4.

61. N. Tcherniak, "Unzere gebildite techter," ibid. 18 (29 Oct. 1902): 2.

of these rights. She attributed their detachment from Zionist activity to the issue with which this chapter began: the failure of Jews, both Orthodox and assimilated, to provide an appropriate Jewish education for their daughters. Jewish women of her day, she noted with regret, "lacked a feeling—the feeling of Jewishness [der khush-hayahadus], the Jewish spark—that the simple kheyder, for all its faults, had implanted in children." She expressed her conviction, as a Zionist and an educator, that politically and socially mature Jewish women would recognize that the Jewish question, and with it the woman question, would be solved only through self-determination— a popular slogan in 1918—and not through assimilation. To achieve this double goal she called upon women to found and lead a national Jewish women's organization with branches throughout Poland and to agitate for the realization of the Poalei-Zion platform plank in support of women's suffrage in Jewish communal elections. This appeal, by an avowed secular Jewish nationalist, was couched in terms that appealed specifically to Jewish pride. "It is not possible," claimed Rakowski, "that we Jews, who were the first bearers of democratic principles, should in this regard lag behind all civilized peoples and close the way for women to achievement of equal rights and to the first step in that direction—to participation in the community."[62]

By the 1920s Rakowski's vision of a national Jewish women's movement apparently was realized in the Jewish Women's Association, though the extent of its reach is unknown. At the very least a cadre of Jewish feminist activists existed. Cen-

62. Puah Rakowska (the Polish form of Rakowski), Di yiddishe froy (Warsaw: Bnos Tsiyon, 1918). The material in this paragraph is drawn from pp. 11–15, 28–29. The quotations are from pp. 14 and 28.

tered in Warsaw, they published pamphlets in Yiddish, among them Di moderne froyen-bavegung (The modern women's movement), under the imprint of the "Publishing House of the Jewish Women's Association in Poland." Two newspapers, one entitled Froyen-shtim (Women's voice) and the other Di froy (The woman), also appeared briefly in the middle of the decade.[63] Unlike the pre-war Froyenvelt, these two women's journals featured primarily female authors and proclaimed the importance of what we may call female self-emancipation. The weekly Di froy explicitly stated in its introductory lead article that "recently Jewish women have also taken it upon themselves to build their own organizations" and therefore needed their own paper. "The Jewish woman," it announced, "must lead a double struggle as a woman from an oppressed and persecuted people." Recognizing that "new modern life demanded a new modern woman," the paper saw its mission as meeting Jewish women's need for contact with the broader world, for learning and independence, while fulfilling their desire to sustain "the sweet, beloved Jewish home with its . . . unassuming traditions of modesty characteristic of the Jewish woman of old."[64] To negotiate this program, framed to appeal to a broad audience by suggesting the need to confront change without sacrificing all traditional values, Di froy planned "to illuminate and to solve all the questions . . . of relevance to the woman in general and the Jewish woman in particular."

63. Puah Rakowska, Di moderne froyen-bavegung (Warsaw, 1928); another pamphlet, by Rokhl Kaplan-Merminski, entitled Froyen-problem, appeared in 1927. I have found two issues of the monthly Froyen-shtim—1 (May 1925) and 2 (Aug. 1925)—and four of Di froy (Apr.–May 1925). Di froy included the cities Vilna, Warsaw, Lodz, and Lemberg (Lvov) on its masthead.

64. Di froy 1 (8 Apr. 1925): 1.

As for general women's issues, the paper proposed to cover the political and economic demands of the woman, her role in culture, literature, art, music, sport, and fashion, and the defense of women's rights. Affirming the importance of the Jewish family, it included in its mandate questions of love and family life, child rearing, and hygiene. Finally, its specific Jewish orientation was Zionist as well as feminist, indicated by its proposed focus on pioneering in Palestine and the building of a new life based on Jewish national culture.[65]

The *Froyen-shtim*, a monthly published by the Jewish Women's Association in Warsaw and coedited by Puah Rakowski, Rokhl Stein, and Leah Proshanski, called upon its readers to assume an active role in political and social activity in this period of change: "In the creation of new ways of life the woman must everywhere take the same part as the man." To supplement existing organizations that contributed to the social development of women, the paper undertook a propaganda campaign of "enlightenment work among Jewish women, because the doors of the Yiddish press are for us women closed with seven locks, . . . to awaken . . . the Jewish woman to take her fate in her own hands, herself to demand and defend her rights. For those of us who can speak . . . our journal offers the opportunity for their voice to be heard."[66]

Jewish feminists sought to persuade their female audience that they had to organize to make their needs known, for the major Jewish political options of the time regularly subordinated women's issues to their central goal, whether that be socialist revolution or nation building in Palestine. Pointing to the international women's movement, feminists argued that

65. Ibid., p. 2.
66. Froyen-shtim 1 (May 1925): 3–4.

86

women shared similar problems throughout the industrial world. These could be solved, in Poland as elsewhere, only through women organizing on their own behalf to secure civic and political equality, equal right to work and equal pay, and equal opportunities for education. Within the Jewish community women had to assume leadership roles and not be limited to working under male direction. Full equality for women within communal institutions, argued one writer in Di froy, was not merely an issue of women's rights but of elementary human rights.[67] One pamphlet highlighted the suffering of Jewish women from syphilis and called upon an unusual triad of doctors, rabbis, and socialists to address the problem.[68] Other feminist writings dealt with issues of specifically Jewish concern, such as the problem of the agunah, the chained wife unable to remarry because she could not acquire a valid Jewish divorce, or the question of the struggle for women's suffrage in Palestine.[69] "The Jewish woman," wrote one activist, Rokhl Kaplan-Merminski, "was . . . wounded on three fronts: as a woman, as a Jew, and as a human being." Celebrating woman's potential for effective social action, she concluded her pamphlet with a powerful combination of radical rhetoric and Jewish imagery: "Let woman rise up! She is going to pluck the apple from the Tree of Life."[70]

67. Rakowska, Di moderne froyen-bavegung, pp. 6–23; Basia Lockerman, "Oyf der vokh," Di froy 2 (1 May 1925): 25–28.

68. Kaplan-Merminski, Froyen-problem, pp. 13–16.

69. On the agunah, see Froyen-shtim 1 (May 1925): 27–28, and Leah Proshanski, "Vegn farlozene froyen" (About abandoned wives), ibid. 2 (Aug. 1925): 10–11; on women's suffrage in Palestine, see Puah Rakowski, "Der kamf far froyen-val-recht in Erets-Yisroel" (The struggle for women's right to vote in the land of Israel), ibid. 2 (Aug. 1925): 4–5.

70. Kaplan-Merminski, Froyen-problem, p. 20.

As a 1928 mimeographed circular letter to its members indicates, the Jewish Women's Association took the message
of social action seriously. The organization particularly addressed the social problems of women and children. During
the summer it ran camps for children and youth; throughout
the year it administered a home for more than fifty poor children and provided vocational courses to enable young girls to
become economically self-sufficient. It also pursued international contacts in dealing with abandoned wives. But it saw its
mission as more than philanthropic. Imbued with the notion
that education led to empowerment, the association also provided instruction for youth in Jewish history and literature,
Polish literature, and sociology; well-attended literacy courses
for illiterate women "of the lower classes"; and public lectures
on literature, politics, and current events. It also sponsored
Palestine-centered work. Seeking greater involvement of its
members, the association's secretary, Puah Rakowski, pointed
out that activity in the organization led to self-education; it
was up to members to lead the way in "work of enlightenment and development." Toward that end, she encouraged
members to set up groups for self-development, for which
the association would provide the necessary literary and bib-
liographic material.[71]

Although they were concerned about the issue of Jewish
women's education or the lack thereof, Jewish leaders in eastern Europe did not cast aspersions upon women until the
interwar years for the defections from traditional practice
that were occurring in their communities. In the Hebrew and

71. Circular letter of the Yudishen Froyen-Ferayn (Jewish Women's Association), Warsaw, 18 Dec. 1928, signed by Puah Rakowska (YIVO Archive,
Poland-Vilna Archive, Warsaw, no. 45).

Yiddish press of the late nineteenth and early twentieth centuries that I surveyed, references to the specific roles of Jewish women and men in the family were few and far between.[72] Jewish commentators aspired to a family life in which women pursued their responsibilities as housewives and mothers unencumbered by the burdens of earning a living—that is, a family life along the lines of the middle and upper classes—but they did not assail Jewish women for their deviation from this bourgeois ideal. In general, women were not blamed for the situation in which they and their families found themselves. Only one signed opinion piece, which appeared in *Der fraynd* in 1913, criticized the reversal of fortune of Jewish men and women. Where once Jewish men had studied while their wives worked to support them, now the women, who were better educated in secular culture and more elegant than their husbands, lived lives of leisure. Whereas the Jewish man had a common language with his son, he had to speak to his daughter in a foreign language, Polish or Russian. "Jewish women," claimed the writer, "were taking revenge on Jewish men for

72. I surveyed *Ahiasaf* (Warsaw), 1893–1904; *Ha-Asif* (Warsaw), 1885–87; *Ben-Ammi* (Saint Petersburg), 1887; *Ha-Boker Or* (Saint Petersburg), 1876, 1896–1903; *Ha-Eshkol* (Cracow), 1898–1903; *Ha-Karmel* (Vilna), 1871–79, irreg.; *Ha-Kerem* (Warsaw), 1887; *Kneset ha-Gedolah* (Warsaw), 1889–92; *Ha-Maggid* (Lyck and later Berlin), 1856–92; *Ha-Meliz* (Odessa and later Saint Petersburg), 1861–72, 1879–1904; *Ha-Mizpeh* (Saint Petersburg), 1885; *Ha-Mizrah* (Cracow), 1903; *Ha-Shahar he-Hadash* (Cracow), 1893; *Ha-Sharon* (Cracow), 1893; *Shem ve-Yafet* (Lvov), 1887; *Ha-Shiloah* (Cracow), 1903–4; *Di naye velt* (Warsaw), 1910; *Der fraynd* (Saint Petersburg), 1913. Further research on the representation of women in Yiddish literature is a major desideratum. For one study, see Ruth Adler, *Women of the Shtetl—Through the Eyes of Y. L. Peretz* (Rutherford, N.J.: Fairleigh Dickinson University Press, 1980), as well as Janet Hadda, *Passionate Women, Passive Men: Suicide in Yiddish Literature* (Albany: State University of New York Press, 1988).

their former sins."[73] Even this article, however, written in a tone of abject self-pity and irony, avoided calling for women to assume responsibilities for Jewish cultural transmission.

In the 1920s, as Jews in Poland became ever more aware of the rapidity of change in the wake of the First World War and as Jewish women began to organize themselves and assert their claim to equal rights within the Jewish community, a few attacks upon women began to appear in the Jewish press, though the economic and political problems confronting Polish Jewry preoccupied newspaper columnists.[74] From female activists' responses in the pages of *Di froy*, it appears that women were criticized for their materialism and love of luxury, faults that were depicted as embittering the lives of their fathers and husbands. Moreover, women were held responsible for the aversion of Jews to productive labor (i.e., noncommercial pursuits)—and also for assimilation. Decrying the generalizations about the assimilationism of Jewish women, one female columnist pointed to the active part that many Jewish women were taking in the Jewish national movement, the renewal of modern Jewish culture, and Jewish social and institutional life.[75] Another asserted that Jewish women should not be blamed for their love of fashion; they were influenced by the surrounding milieu, just as Maimonides had been influenced by the Aristotelian philosophy popular in his own time! Although admitting that there was an "assimilated element" in female Jewish society, such was the

73. *Der fraynd* 47 (24 Feb. 1913): 3.

74. My survey of two popular Yiddish newspapers, *Haynt* and *Der moment*, for 1925 revealed only a handful of articles that dealt with women or the woman's question.

75. Basia Lockerman, "Unzer lage," *Di froy* 1 (8 Apr. 1925): 3–6.

case among men as well. Moreover, in response to the criticism that the language of their people was foreign to women, the writer offered a sophisticated critique of those who would limit culture to elite Hebrew literature alone: "The *tkhines* in Yiddish, the *Taytsh Chumash* (*Tseneurene*), later the novels of Shoymer—all of these were read by women, and from them developed the popular language. The Yiddish language is created not only by writers and literary types but also by the women in the marketplace who find new, original little words to express their feelings."[76]

The late development of a communal debate on the roles of women and the modest scope of that debate when it arose reflect the specific conditions of east European Jewish life. Although many changes occurred among east European Jewry beginning in the last quarter of the nineteenth century, the majority of the Jewish population remained in the first stages of the process of acculturation until the interwar years. The structural features of the societies in which Jews lived limited the possibilities of full assimilation. However secular some Jewish men and women became, their acculturation and social integration were not perceived by most communal spokesmen as a meaningful threat to Jewish group survival. Even secularized Jews were likely to retain a strong ethnic Jewish identity, generated internally and reinforced from without. The problems that communal leaders identified as deserving of immediate attention, therefore, tended not to be issues of assimilation but questions of securing economic and political equality for their vulnerable constituents, of solving the "Jewish problem" through nationalism, socialist revolution, or emigration. Such matters fell in the domain of public

76. "Fraye tribune," ibid. 3 (8 May 1925): 48–49.

policy, from which both Jewish and general society tended to exclude women and their particular concerns.

Insofar as assimilation was itself a secondary issue, the question of women remained marginal. Jewish leaders in eastern Europe recognized the need to mobilize women to support the broad economic, political, and ideological programs that flourished in their communities, as was reflected in their concern about the nature of women's education. But in eastern Europe women were not perceived as the linchpin of cultural transmission, as they were in the West. Through their migration westward, however, east European Jews would contribute to the ongoing debate about women's roles in constructing and sustaining modern Judaism and the modern Jewish community.

# 3

## America, Freedom, and Assimilation

"I thought it [a] miracle . . . that I, Mashke, the granddaughter of Raphael the Russian, born to a humble destiny, should be at home in an American metropolis, be free to fashion my own life, and should dream my dreams in English phrases."[1] So wrote Mary Antin in her well-received 1912 book, *The Promised Land*. Precociously publishing her autobiography at the age of thirty, Antin celebrated her new American homeland with these words of elation. Through the gift of free public education, America offered her the opportunity to remake herself. In the process, as she was careful to point out in a period of growing anti-immigrant sentiment, America was enriched by the talents of newcomers such as herself, quick to cast off the baggage of their European origins and to contribute to American society. America was "the promised land" for Jewish immigrants irrespective of gender, but women appear to have been particularly attuned to the possibilities of renegotiating the norms that governed their access to education as well as their behavior in the public realms of work, leisuretime activities, and politics. America permitted the continual rethinking of the boundaries between the domestic and the public spheres.

Between 1880 and 1914 almost two million Jews from eastern Europe, of whom 43 percent were women, settled in the

1. Mary Antin, *The Promised Land* (1912; reprint, Boston: Houghton-Mifflin, 1969), p. 197.

United States.[2] Like most immigrants, they saw in America
an opportunity to escape the grim poverty of their regions
of birth, primarily the Russian Pale of Settlement, but also
Galicia and Romania. Even those less starry-eyed than Mary
Antin about the wonders of urban America recognized the
need to accommodate to American conditions. They considered assimilation to be a natural concomitant of the decision
to migrate.

Although the process of assimilation seemed inevitable to
immigrants, the project of assimilation was complicated by
the struggle of American elites with the potential impact of
mass immigration on the definition of American identity. During the years in which immigrant Jews from eastern Europe
confronted America, different concepts of Americanization
competed for public attention. For some, Americanization necessitated Anglo-conformity, the abandonment of immigrant
mores in favor of far-reaching assimilation to an American
culture defined by its English roots. For others, who preferred
the image of the "melting pot," Americanization demanded
assimilation, but American society and culture themselves
would be transformed through the incorporation of various
immigrant groups. Between 1915 and 1925 Horace Kallen, an
American professor of Jewish immigrant origins, developed
a third approach to Americanization, which promoted the
ideal of cultural pluralism. That doctrine presumed that immigrants and their descendants would retain aspects of their
cultures of origin even as they acculturated. American society

2. Kuznets, "Immigration of Russian Jews to the United States," pp.
94–95.

and culture would be a federation of the diverse ethnic groups that composed the country's population.[3]

Because of their immediate needs and aspirations, immigrant Jews paid little attention to the competing doctrines of Americanization. They were so little concerned with countering assimilation that they preferred to rely upon public education rather than to found Jewish parochial schools. In fact, in immigrant communities most Jewish children received no Jewish education at all, though sons were more likely than daughters to have some traditional Jewish instruction. David Blaustein, a prominent Jewish social worker and director of the Educational Alliance, the most important Jewish settlement house on the Lower East Side, reported in 1904 that in the 307 khadorim of the district there were 8,616 male students—and 361 females. Consequently, the Alliance set up special religious classes for girls, although they met only three times a week, as opposed to five times a week for the boys' classes.[4] Even in 1917 when the young Jewish educator Alexander Dushkin conducted a comprehensive survey of Jewish education in New York City as part of his doctoral dissertation for Columbia University's Teachers College, he found that only 24 percent of the city's Jewish children were enrolled

3. For a discussion of concepts of immigrant assimilation, see John Higham, *Send These to Me: Jews and Other Immigrants in Urban America* (New York: Atheneum, 1975), pp. 196–230. Horace Kallen elaborated his ideas about cultural pluralism in his 1924 book, *Culture and Democracy in the United States* (New York: Boni & Liveright, 1924).

4. David Blaustein, "Preventive Work on the East Side," an address delivered to the National Conference of Jewish Charities, in *Memoirs of David Blaustein: Educator and Communal Worker*, arranged by Miriam Blaustein (New York: McBride, Nast & Co., 1913), pp. 140, 145.

in Jewish Sunday, afternoon, or day schools or had a private tutor. In Jewish schools girls accounted for one-third of the students, but they were far more likely than their brothers to be limited to a Sunday School—rather than a more extensive—Jewish education.[5] Jewish communal references to assimilation in the period of mass migration from eastern Europe emanated for the most part not from the immigrants themselves but from the middle- and upper-class leadership of the established American Jewish community of central European origin. Most of them did not worry about rampant assimilation; rather, they were concerned that the immigrants' assimilation to American ways and values was not rapid and certain enough. From their perspective, speedy Americanization was essential for subverting the growing association in popular opinion of "Jew" with "foreigner."[6] The immigrants, for their part, confronted more-pressing concerns than assimilation: they had to find housing and jobs to provide for the support of their families.

In the early twentieth century, as the children of the immigrants grew to maturity and tension between the generations rose, assimilation became a more highly charged issue than it had been in eastern Europe. But in the immigrant commu-

5. On the 1917 survey, see Alexander M. Dushkin, *Jewish Education in New York City* (New York: Bureau of Jewish Education, 1918), pp. 145–63, 430.

6. On native Jewish attitudes toward the immigrants from eastern Europe, see Zosa Szajkowski, "The Attitude of American Jews to East European Jewish Immigrants," *Publications of the American Jewish Historical Society* 40 (1950–51): 221–80; Esther Panitz, "The Polarity of American Jewish Attitudes towards Immigration (1870–1891)," in *The Jewish Experience in America*, ed. Abraham Karp (Waltham: American Jewish Historical Society, 1969), 4:31–62; and Esther Panitz, "In Defense of the Jewish Immigrant, 1891–1924," in ibid., 5:23–63.

nity in America, as in eastern Europe, women were not the focus of communal blame, although their changed roles and their special responsibility for cultural transmission were duly noted. Likewise, although they aspired to achieve the comforts associated with the middle class, the majority of the immigrant Jewish population was not middle class, and the rigid gender segregation that prevailed in middle-class families was not yet dominant. The values of east European Jewish culture, transplanted to America and gradually transformed by America, permitted women to play a complex role in the accommodation of their families to the conditions of American society.

In some ways Jewish women were agents of assimilation; in others, buffers against the disruptive influences of the new society. The image of the conservative immigrant woman, reluctant to cast off her wig, appeared in English-language immigrant fiction and memoirs.[7] Immigrant daughters have commented on their mothers' contentment with remaining in a "ghetto" milieu, surrounded by Yiddish-speaking neighbors and the familiar sights, sounds, and smells of the culture of their birth. Ida Richter remarked of her mother's reaction to settling on Chicago's West Side: "Those days, my mother was glad to live in a ghetto. She had her friends, her language, she had her synagogue near the house."[8] Yet, as the histo-

7. See, e.g., Rose Cohen, *Out of the Shadow* (New York: George H. Doran Co., 1918), pp. 152–54. Rose, who emigrated to America with her father as an adolescent, persuaded her newly arrived mother to wear her own hair by arguing vigorously that bewigged women looked older and more old-fashioned than their husbands. See also Abraham Cahan, *Yekl: A Tale of the New York Ghetto* (New York: D. Appleton & Co., 1896), pp. 120–22.

8. Sydelle Kramer and Jenny Masur, eds., *Jewish Grandmothers* (Boston: Beacon Press, 1976), p. 129.

rian Andrew Heinze has pointed out in his book *Adapting to Abundance*, the easy availability of consumer goods, promoted by skillful advertising, facilitated Americanization of women as well as men.[9] The new immigrant could easily acquire the external signs of the American, and most exchanged the European clothing of the greenhorn for stylish American garb soon after their arrival. As the family member most responsible for decisions about household purchases, both major and minor, the woman presided over a process of acquisition that provided immigrants with the markers of American identity and mobility—from American food products to a piano for the parlor. Recognizing the role of the wife and mother as consumer, American companies advertised widely in Yiddish in the most-popular immigrant newspapers.[10] Heinze suggests that immigrant Jewish women were particularly adept at strategic consumption because of their extensive experience with the marketplace in their *shtetlach* (towns) and cities of origin.

Urban America offered countless leisure-time pursuits, including shopping, to immigrant Jewish women, far more than had been available to them in the towns and cities of eastern Europe. New styles of clothing and new types of recreation fostered a self-conscious separation of the immigrant from the Old Country and an assertion of American identity. Fashion lured Jewish working girls, especially those employed in

9. Andrew Heinze, *Adapting to Abundance: Jewish Immigrants, Mass Consumption, and the Search for American Identity* (New York: Columbia University Press, 1990).

10. For examples, see Jenna Weissman Joselit, "'A Set Table': Jewish Domestic Culture in the New World, 1880–1950," in *Getting Comfortable in New York: The American Jewish Home, 1880–1950*, ed. Susan L. Braunstein and Jenna Weissman Joselit (New York: Jewish Museum, 1990), pp. 36–37.

the garment industry. One immigrant woman recalled of her youth and her attraction to American fashion: "We used to love the American people, to copy them. I wanted to be an American very much. I saw people who looked better and dressed better and I wanted to be like [them]."[11] Immigrant working daughters often expressed the sense of freedom that wages conferred upon them by withholding a portion of their salaries for their own use and treating themselves to the latest fashions or purchasing luxuries for their homes.[12] One Gentile New England woman noted this tendency in a 1905 article about immigrant Jews:

> The young girl, impulsive, warmhearted, attractive and thoroughly modest, with her yearnings for things pretty and dainty, and refined [in] her taste for domesticity is a quickwitted agent in bringing the amenities of the American home into the beautiful Jewish family life. Her estimate of what these amenities may be comes mostly through her romantic reading, her experience as a shop girl, and her frequent indulgence in the theater.[13]

Like their fellow workers, immigrant Jewish women also frequented the dance halls, movies, and amusement parks that provided leisure-time diversion to working-class youth

11. Ida Richter, "The Entrepreneur/Raconteur," in *Jewish Grandmothers*, ed. Kramer and Masur, p. 130; also cited in Glenn, *Daughters of the Shtetl*, pp. 160–61.

12. Sydney Stahl Weinberg, *The World of Our Mothers: The Lives of Jewish Immigrant Women* (Chapel Hill: University of North Carolina Press, 1988), pp. 187–92.

13. Emmelyn Foster Peck, "The Russian Jew in Southern New England," *New England Magazine*, n.s., 31 (1904–5): 32, as cited in Rudolf Glanz, *The Jewish Woman in America*, vol. 1, *The Eastern European Jewish Woman* (n.p.: Ktav Publishing House and National Council of Jewish Women, 1976), p. 86.

when their day's labor was concluded.[14] Even when they remained within ethnic enclaves on the Lower East Side or in similar neighborhoods in other cities and sought particularly Jewish forms of recreation, they spent their time in coffeehouses or at the Yiddish theater rather than in their crowded tenement apartments.[15] Through inexpensive recreation and entertainment that took place outside the confines of the family, turn-of-the-century urban America promoted heterosocial contact, which challenged immigrant parents' presumptions about gender relations. To their children, however, the unchaperoned socializing of young men and women who met at work or in dance halls or through friends became widely accepted as a signifier of the freedom that America conferred on youth. Although middle- and upper-class social reformers criticized the dance halls in particular, which they saw as breeding grounds for prostitution, and sought to provide supervised settings for mixed entertainment, they failed to divert girls from commercial dancing establishments to socials organized by settlement houses or other nonprofit organizations. Belle Israels (later, Moskowitz) was one such reformer—a member of the Committee of Fourteen (a civic association seeking to stamp out prostitution), chairperson of the Committee on Amusements and Vacation Resources of Working Girls, and an activist with the Educational Alliance. She ruefully noted, "Of many hundreds of girls spoken to only nine had ever heard of a settlement or church society."[16]

14. Glenn, Daughters of the Shtetl, pp. 158–62; Kathy Peiss, Cheap Amusements: Working Women and Leisure in Turn-of-the-Century New York (Philadelphia: Temple University Press, 1986).

15. On cafés and the theater, see Hutchins Hapgood, The Spirit of the Ghetto (1902; reprint, New York: Schocken Books, 1966), pp. 118–75, 283–87.

16. Belle Israels, "The Way of the Girl," The Survey, 3 July 1909, p. 488,

Immigrant parents often disapproved of their children's new patterns of leisure and courtship, but many tacitly acquiesced to their independence. Parents realized that as strangers to American mores they could not strictly regulate their wage-earning children's behavior in adolescence and young adulthood. Some historians argue that Jewish parents were less restrictive than immigrant parents of other ethnic groups.[17] And in many cases parents were no longer authorities to be reckoned with, since they remained in the Old Country. Thus, Ruth Katz, who emigrated to the United States without her parents in 1913 at the age of sixteen, had a very different social experience from her older sisters, whose marriages were arranged in Russia. Ruth described the rituals of her own five-year courtship, which began a year after she arrived in Chicago: "We bought a nickel ice cream cone; for twenty-five cents we went to Jackson Park and you took a boat for an hour. . . . Sometimes, when you were more serious with a girl, you took her out Wednesday for a movie. . . . Who was chaperoned? Not in this country."[18]

Although immigrant Jewish working girls, like their peers in other immigrant groups, became Americanized through shopping and mixed recreational activity, they saw in education the most significant, though often frustratingly unattain-

as cited by Beth Wenger, "'Girls Need to Dance': Virtue and Vice in the Jewish Quarter" (Yale University, unpublished paper). On the career of Belle Israels Moskowitz, see Elisabeth Israels Perry, Belle Moskowitz: Feminine Politics and the Exercise of Power in the Age of Alfred E. Smith (New York: Oxford University Press, 1987), esp. pp. 3–22, 67–69.

17. Elizabeth Ewen, Immigrant Women in the Land of Dollars: Life and Culture on the Lower East Side, 1890–1925 (New York: Monthly Review Press, 1985), p. 208; Peiss, Cheap Amusements, pp. 68–69.

18. Kramer and Masur, eds., Jewish Grandmothers, pp. 146–47.

able, element of American freedom. Sharing the Jewish passion for learning and aware of the double discrimination they had faced as Jewish girls in eastern Europe—excluded from traditional forms of Jewish learning as females and limited in their access to public education as Jews—they dreamed of sitting in America's free public schools. As "Fannie Shapiro," who arrived in the United States from Belorussia in 1906 as an adolescent, put it in an interview in her old age: "And I told my parents, 'I want to go to America. I want to learn, I want to see a life, and I want to go to school.'"[19] Like most adolescent immigrants, however, including Mary Antin's older sister Frieda, "Fannie Shapiro" did not gain access to the public education that set Mary Antin on her path to fame and assimilation. She had to go to work in a garment shop to support herself, and she found herself so tired after ten hours at the sewing machine that she fell asleep during night classes.[20]

Communal values, however, supported children's staying in school even when that situation created family hardship. In 1907 a Jewish Daily Forward editor, in the paper's popular advice column, "A Bintel Brief," advised a fourteen-year-old girl who expressed her reluctance to remain in school because of the family's poverty that she should obey her parents, who were willing to sacrifice so that she might continue her education. In doing so, she would give them nakhes (a com-

19. Pseudonymous interview, in ibid., p. 8.

20. Ibid., pp. 10–11. For a general assessment of the desire of immigrant Jewish girls and their parents for education and of the economic difficulties that often prevented the attainment of their goals, see Weinberg, The World of Our Mothers, pp. 167–83. Weinberg has pointed out that access to education depended primarily on birth order, with younger children of immigrants having greater opportunities for schooling, and only secondarily on gender.

bination of pride, satisfaction, and comfort), which would outweigh her possible contribution to the meager household budget.[21] Despite the difficulties of attending school after a long day's work, many young immigrant Jewish women did learn English and expanded their secular education through free adult education evening classes. Their struggle for education is reflected poignantly in a 1910 letter to the "Bintel Brief" written by a married woman with small children who attended evening high school two nights a week, much to the consternation of her husband, who regularly kept her standing outside when she rang the bell upon her return home. To force her to abandon her studies, he had introduced a new regulation:

> Because I send out the laundry to be done, it seems to him that I have too much time for myself, even enough to go to school. So from now on he will count every penny . . . so I will not be able to send out the laundry any more. And when I have to do the work myself there won't be any time left for such "foolishness" as going to school. I told him that I'm willing to do my own washing but that I would still be able to find time for study. . . . The fact that he is intelligent makes me more annoyed with him. He is in favor of the emancipation of women, yet in real life he acts contrary to his beliefs.

In response to the woman's doubts about the correctness of her position, the editor encouraged her to persevere and strongly chastised her husband.[22]

In her semi-autobiographical novels, Anzia Yezierska, the only immigrant Jewish woman writer to achieve fame, albeit

21. I. Metzker, ed., *A Bintel Brief* (Garden City, N.Y.: Doubleday, 1971), pp. 70–71.

22. Ibid., pp. 109–10.

fleeting, in the 1920s, placed the struggle for education at the center of her heroines' quests to become American.[23] Like Yezierska herself, her female protagonists deprive themselves of food and adequate lodging and work at menial jobs in order to acquire secular learning. The availability of education because of their migration represents America to them. By studying they signify their repudiation of the cultural backwardness and female subordination they associate with the traditional Judaism and east European ways of their parents in favor of an "American aesthetic."[24] Even those women who succeed, however, recognize that they can never become fully American because of their family ties and origins; they are caught between two worlds. Some of her heroines, like Sara Smolinsky in *Bread Givers*, come to acknowledge the connection between their own will to education and stubborn perseverance and the culture and personality of their parents, in this case Sara's fanatically orthodox father, who had dubbed her "*blut und eisen* [blood and iron]."[25]

23. On Yezierska, see her daughter's biography, Louise Levitas Henriksen (with the assistance of Jo Ann Boydston), *Anzia Yezierska: A Writer's Life* (New Brunswick: Rutgers University Press, 1986), as well as the novels and stories listed in the Bibliography. Yezierska was "rediscovered" in the 1970s as a result of the growing interest in women's history and literature stimulated by the emergence of the second wave of feminism.

24. Ellen Golub, "Eat Your Heart Out: The Fiction of Anzia Yezierska," in *Jewish Women Writers and Women in Jewish Literature: Studies in American Jewish Literature*, vol. 3, ed. Daniel Walden (Albany: State University of New York Press, 1983), p. 58.

25. Anzia Yezierska, *Bread Givers* (Garden City, N.Y.: Doubleday, Doran, 1925; reprint, New York: Persea Books, 1975), p. 279. W. H. Auden commented upon the similarity in temperament between Yezierska and the father she describes in her fiction in his introduction to her purported

Although many economic obstacles stood in the way of education, large numbers of immigrant Jewish women received sufficient communal and familial support to realize at least some of their goals. In two sociological studies, one published in 1914 and the other in 1930, Gentile observers commented on the disproportionately large number of Jewish women among the students in evening courses. In Philadelphia in 1925, for example, Jewish women accounted for 70 percent of the night-school students![26] Moreover, in the 1920s immigrant Jewish daughters were more likely to attend high school and college than the daughters of other ethnic groups. Estimates suggest that by 1934 more than 50 percent of female college students in New York were Jewish, although Jews constituted less than a third of New York's population.[27] In addition to formal classes, immigrant women also attended the myriad lectures sponsored by organizations with political interests, such as unions or the Workmen's Circle (a Yiddish socialist cultural society), and by settlement houses. In 1904, for example, the *Settlement Journal* noted: "The girls have not omitted to take advantage of the many opportunities offered them to listen to lectures on politics and economics. Indeed, for the last three years the girls have taken part in debates with

---

autobiography, *Red Ribbon on a White Horse* (New York: Charles Scribner's Sons, 1950), p. 22.

26. Mary Van Kleeck, *Working Girls in Evening Schools: A Statistical Study* (New York: Survey Associates, 1914); Caroline Manning, *The Immigrant Woman and Her Job* (Washington: U.S. Government Printing Office, 1930), with the Philadelphia information found on p. 27.

27. Leonard Dinnerstein, "Education and the Advancement of American Jews," in *American Education and the European Immigrant*, ed. Bernard Weiss (Urbana: University of Illinois Press, 1981), p. 47.

the boys on these subjects."[28] With its dance halls and amusement parks, lectures and evening schools, America offered immigrant Jewish women the freedom to experiment with an array of public secular activities.

Jewish reformers and social workers, generally descendants of central European Jews of an earlier migration, sought to curtail that freedom through their provision of philanthropic assistance to the most needy of Jewish immigrants and through the organization of leisure-time activity. Firmly anchored in the middle and upper classes, they shared the assumptions of others of their social status about order and civility. They presumed that the children of the urban immigrant working classes were in need of supervision and instruction in the values of self-discipline, punctuality, and cleanliness, which their parents were unable to provide. Like other progressive reformers, they were convinced that the urban working-class environment was dangerous for youth and would prevent the inculcation of the values essential for civic rectitude and responsible, moral adult behavior.[29] Yet, they were also genuinely concerned with helping immigrant Jews make their way in America and experience the upward mobility that had been their own lot. Their concern was heightened by their awareness that their own status and image were linked in the public imagination with the Yiddish-speaking newcomers. It was therefore in their interest to pro-

28. On the immigrant Jewish passion for lectures, see *Settlement Journal* 1, no. 1 (Apr. 1904): p. 3, as cited in Glanz, *The Jewish Woman in America*, 1:40.

29. On the urban "youth problem" that emerged in public perception at the turn of the twentieth century and the use of education, formal and informal, to combat it, see David Nasaw, *Schooled to Order: A Social History of Public Schooling in the United States* (New York: Oxford University Press, 1979), pp. 87–104.

mote behavior that would reflect well upon all Jews. As respectable members of the middle and upper classes, Jewish social workers, reformers, and philanthropists were particularly sensitive to the mores and image of women, for an entire group's honor could be called into question by the disreputable conduct of its women—hence, the extraordinary anxiety of established American Jews about the participation of immigrant Jews in "white slavery" and the potential of dance halls as recruiting grounds for prostitution.[30]

In their institutions and programs Jewish leaders concerned with the Americanization of the immigrants targeted immigrant Jewish girls for socialization in respectability and in class and gender deference. The Educational Alliance, for example, established different types of programs for boys and for girls. Whereas boys had to participate in athletics and were encouraged to compete with teams from other settlement houses, so that they might refute the charge that Jewish men were physically weak and lacked courage, girls were enrolled in more-demure activities. They were taught domestic skills so that they might, in the words of the Educational Alliance Annual Report of 1902, "cultivate a taste for those domestic virtues that tend to make home-life happier and brighter."[31] David Blaustein, the director of the Alliance, was concerned with bridging the gap between immigrant parents and their children and recognized the need to preserve certain aspects of east European Jewish culture. Because he sought to re-

30. On Jews and prostitution, see Bristow, *Prostitution and Prejudice.*

31. Cary Goodman, *Choosing Sides: Playground and Street Life on the Lower East Side* (New York: Schocken Books, 1979), pp. 37–39. The quotation is from the Educational Alliance Annual Report of 1902, p. 21 (cited in Goodman, *Choosing Sides,* p. 38).

inforce familial ties, he did not use Alliance classes to introduce the latest American ideas about the New Woman. In a public address he remarked that he avoided the temptation to use education to "transform [the Jewish woman] into what may be called a new being, giving her a new conception of the position of the woman in the home."[32] In this gender differentiation the Educational Alliance followed the prevailing view of the organized-play movement, whose national association, the Playground Association of America, established in 1906, "developed programs for the playgrounds, schools, and recreation centers that would 'make boys more manly and girls more womanly.'"[33] The purpose of physical activity for girls was to teach them poise and grace; strenuous games like basketball, field hockey, and all track competition were deemed inappropriate for females.

Institutions sponsored by Jewish philanthropists that were explicitly designed to provide vocational education also promoted a curriculum for girls determined by a combination of class- and gender-bound values. The Clara de Hirsch Home for Working Girls, for example (a boardinghouse and vocational school founded in 1897 by two members of New York City's German Jewish elite and by Baroness Clara de Hirsch), recognized that its residents, or inmates as they were called, needed to be able to support themselves through wage labor, but it limited its training to skills that were not only marketable but also necessary for women in their role as homemaker.[34] The

32. "The Problem of Immigration in the United States," an address delivered to the City Club of Chicago, 1909, in *Memoirs of David Blaustein*, p. 170.

33. Ibid., p. 132. The citation is from the psychologist G. Stanley Hall, *Youth—Its Education, Regimen, and Hygiene* (New York: Appleton, 1906), p. 284.

34. The information in this paragraph is drawn from Nancy B. Sinkoff,

Clara de Hirsch Home therefore concentrated on instruction in hand and machine sewing, dressmaking, and millinery, as well as offering a course in domestic service that taught the arts of cooking, laundry, and serving. Although the formal domestic service training program was discontinued in 1902 due to lack of interest (i.e., resistance on the part of the immigrant women themselves), the Clara de Hirsch Home offered evening classes in cooking and sewing to its residents and promulgated Jewish religious values and celebrations in the spirit of Reform Judaism. It also provided chaperoned social events, enforced a curfew, and in 1915 introduced lectures in sex hygiene in order to limit the sexual experimentation of its boarders. The directors of the home saw all these activities as central to their mission of preparing their charges for their ultimate vocation as wives and mothers. Rose Sommerfeld, the "Resident Directress" of the home, declared at the 1906 meeting of the National Conference of Jewish Charities that "we really believe salvation for the working girl lies in the fact of being married and having a home of her own. . . . We do train them so that when they do get married, they will be the right sort of home makers."[35] Americanization of young immigrant women, as Jewish reformers understood it, entailed adoption of American middle-class gendered norms and values.

Jewish-sponsored settlement houses and educational organizations were limited in their influence. For most immigrants who came in contact with them, they were only sup-

"Educating for 'Proper' Jewish Womanhood: A Case Study in Domesticity and Vocational Training, 1897–1926," *American Jewish History* 77, no. 4 (June 1988): 572–99.

35. Cited in ibid., p. 593.

plementary to more-powerful institutions. The world of wage labor had the greatest impact on the assimilation of young, unmarried Jewish women immigrants. Although married Jewish women shunned employment in factory and workshop to a much greater extent than immigrant women of other ethnic groups in favor of taking in boarders or "helping" in family businesses,[36] most immigrant Jewish women worked for several years before marriage, primarily in the garment industry. The historian Susan Glenn has found that they preferred larger factories, with their more-cosmopolitan atmosphere, to smaller workshops and approached the world of work differently from men. Because the gendered division of labor and wages within the industry limited their opportunities for advancement and because they expected that employment in shop or factory would occupy only a few years of their lives, women viewed economic success less in terms of personal achievement than as part of a familial strategy of mobility, even though they still valued accomplishment on the job.[37] Although immigrant daughters expected to hand over much of their wages to their families, earning a salary and deciding precisely how much to contribute to the family budget reinforced American notions of independence.[38] As early as 1902 one Gentile observer noted "an unusual development of independent initiative on the part of the young Jewish shop

36. Paula E. Hyman, "Gender and the Immigrant Jewish Experience in the United States," in *Jewish Women in Historical Perspective*, ed. Judith R. Baskin (Detroit: Wayne State University Press, 1991), pp. 225–27; Glenn, *Daughters of the Shtetl*, pp. 72–77.

37. Glenn, *Daughters of the Shtetl*, pp. 90–131, esp. pp. 124–25.

38. Weinberg, *World of Our Mothers*, pp. 190–91.

girl."[39] That sense of independence has been confirmed in numerous oral histories. As one immigrant Jewish woman put it, "The best part was when I got a job for myself and was able to stand on my own feet."[40] The experience of Jewish women at work also introduced them to union issues and socialist ideas, which they continued to espouse well after they had left the ranks of the employed.

As women's historians have noted, work outside the home in and of itself does not necessarily lead to politicization. Prevailing social and political attitudes within the family are more important in predicting women's level of political activism than is work history.[41] The norms of east European Jewish culture that had permitted women to play a role in the secular public sphere as well as women's premigration experience with work and politics were crucial in determining Jewish women's role in the American immigrant community, fostering an openness to issues beyond their domestic concerns. Women who had been active in the Bund in Russia, for example, generally continued their socialist commitments when they immigrated to America and found appropriate vehicles to express their ideals. Esther Luria, a Bund member and radical intellectual, published more than sixty articles on socialist-

39. Mabel Hurd Willett, *The Employment of Women in the Clothing Trade* (1902; New York: AMS Press, 1928), pp. 87–88, as cited in Weinberg, *World of Our Mothers*, p. 191.

40. Cited in Corinne Azen Krause, "Urbanization without Breakdown: Italian, Jewish, and Slavic Immigrant Women in Pittsburgh," *Journal of Urban History* 4, no. 3 (1978): 296.

41. Ibid; see also Virginia Yans-McLaughlin, *Family and Community: Italian Immigrants in Buffalo, 1880–1930* (Ithaca: Cornell University Press, 1977), esp. pp. 202–15.

feminist themes in the socialist monthly *Tsukunft* and in the International Ladies' Garment Workers' Union weekly paper *Glaykhhayt* between 1912 and the early 1920s.[42] Luria was exceptional in her level of educational achievement—she held a doctorate from a Swiss university—and in her degree of politicization. However, more-typical working-class women were also active in political and social causes, albeit in a less-intellectual capacity. American social reformers who commented upon a wide range of immigrant women noted that Jewish women were far more attuned to political questions and far more convinced of their right to act politically than were their immigrant neighbors and shopmates of different ethnic origins.[43] Jewish women's sense of the appropriateness of their behavior was derived from the cultural message about women's roles conveyed within their families and in such organs of Jewish public opinion as the Yiddish press. The immigrant Jewish community repeatedly expressed its support of women's activism, rallying behind the female-initiated and female-led kosher meat boycott of 1902, the female-led rent strikes, and the women participants in the garment strike of 1909.[44] In his 1924 history of the International Ladies' Garment Workers' Union, Louis Levine asserted that the women's 1909 strike, the Uprising of the 20,000, "laid the foundations of unionism in the dress and waist trade . . . and inspired the workers in other branches of the industry." Further, he

42. Norma Fain Pratt, "Transitions in Judaism: The Jewish American Woman through the 1930s," *American Quarterly* 30 (1978): 689.

43. Mary Van Kleeck, *Artificial Flower Makers* (New York: Survey Associates, 1913), pp. 34–35.

44. On the kosher meat boycott, see Paula E. Hyman, "Immigrant Women and Consumer Protest: The New York Kosher Meat Boycott of 1902," *American Jewish History* 70, no. 1 (Sept. 1980): 91–105.

was not reluctant to acknowledge that "though the principal union officials were men and the direction of the strike was in the hands of men, the women played a preponderant part in carrying it through. It was mainly women who did the picketing, who were arrested and fined, who ran the risk of assault, who suffered ill-treatment from the police and the courts."[45] As one observer put it with pride, the strike activists were "unzere vunderbare farbrente meydlekh [our wonderful fervent girls]."[46] The immigrant Jewish community also supported women's suffrage at the polls in New York City in the state elections of 1915 and 1917 more than any other immigrant group. Although it was women who provided sustained community organizing on this issue and dedicated themselves to getting out the vote, Jewish men were enormously receptive to the women's message.[47]

Historian Maxine Seller has demonstrated that the women's page of the Jewish Daily Forward, the most popular Yiddish paper in America, reinforced the acceptance of female participation in the world of work and politics. Unlike the English-language press, the Forward did not presume that women's interests could be contained within the areas of fashion and

45. Louis Levine, The Women's Garment Workers: A History of the International Ladies' Garment Workers' Union (New York: B. W. Huebsch, 1924), pp. 166, 156.

46. As cited in Irving Howe, World of Our Fathers: The Journey of the East European Jews to America and the Life They Found and Made (New York: Simon & Schuster, 1976), p. 300.

47. On the issue of women's suffrage, see Elinor Lerner, "Jewish Involvement in the New York City Woman Suffrage Movement," American Jewish History 70, no. 4 (1981): 444–53. On the women labor activists, see Charlotte Baum, Paula Hyman, and Sonya Michel, The Jewish Woman in America (New York: Dial Press, 1976), pp. 121–62, Howe, World of Our Fathers, pp. 295–300, and, most recently, Glenn, Daughters of the Shtetl, pp. 167–206.

home economics. Rather, its editors constructed a secular, moderately socialist vision of Jewish womanhood, providing information on politics, the labor movement, and the international women's movement and calling for women to participate in all three areas.[48] This communal acceptance of women as active subjects, rather than passive objects, of history recognized, and promoted, the status of women as partners in negotiating the public role of Jews in American society.

Despite their endorsement of women's public roles, most immigrant Jewish leaders also acknowledged that women's primary influence was within the home. Jewish leaders instructed immigrant housewives in rearing their American children and suggested means for creating intergenerational harmony. In the 1910s and 1920s immigrants in American cities had available a wealth of books and journals in Yiddish that offered advice on subjects as varied as hygiene, table manners, sexuality, fashion, parenting, and birth control.[49] Some books were written expressly for the immigrant audience; others, such as Margaret Sanger's influential pamphlet *What Every Girl Should Know*, were translated into Yiddish. The journal *Unzer gezund* (Our health), for example, first published in 1910, provided progressive information on aspects of what we might describe as preventive medicine, such as the importance of fresh air and adequate ventilation. Although we can-

48. Maxine S. Seller, "Defining Socialist Womanhood: The Women's Page of the *Jewish Daily Forward* in 1919," *American Jewish History* 76, no. 4 (1987): 416–38.

49. For a sophisticated discussion of this literature as a mirror of Jewish immigrant culture in America, see Eli Lederhendler, "Guides for the Perplexed: Sex, Manners, and Mores for the Yiddish Reader in America," *Modern Judaism* 11, no. 3 (Oct. 1991): 321–41. The information in this paragraph is drawn from Lederhendler's essay.

not know how immigrant readers responded to this material, the popularity of Sanger's pamphlet, which was repeatedly reprinted, and of books of etiquette suggests that immigrants sought to familiarize themselves with the new options and expectations of life in America.

These advice manuals, books, and journals were overwhelmingly secular in their orientation. Their goal was to help their readers adapt to the conditions that confronted them in their new homes. Jewish identity, it was assumed, would take care of itself. Indeed, the advice literature presumed that migration necessitated a break with the culture of the Old Country, that it offered the welcome possibility of liberation from traditional constraints. The advice manuals also recognized that immigrant Jews sought to achieve middle-class status, and thus, immigrant men and women would have to be educated in the niceties of middle-class social behavior. By learning good manners, immigrant Jews would become good Americans and would earn the respect of Gentile society.[50]

Although the task of adapting to middle-class American standards of good taste fell upon both men and women, advice literature tended to address women on specific issues more often than men. The popular Yiddish book *Etikete*, written by an Orthodox journalist under the pseudonym Tashrak, focused upon female fashion lapses, for example. "It is dreadful what bad taste most of our Jewish girls have," he noted. Presumably the self-presentation of women through their style of dress and behavior was a primary marker of American social status. Tashrak also called upon Jewish women to avoid the path of the modern women's movement, which confused "freedom with permissiveness." Instead he promoted a tradi-

50. Ibid., pp. 330–33.

tional view of women's needs and of male-female relations. "For thousands of years," he proclaimed with approbation, "woman has been the weaker sex, dependent upon man, abandoned to his protection. . . . The greatest, most prominent, and most educated woman wants a husband who will be, at least in some respects, superior to her." Although men and women theoretically enjoyed equal rights and marriage was a partnership, Tashrak concluded, surprisingly with an expression of regret, that, in reality, the husband—the breadwinner—was the boss (*balebos*).[51]

Advice literature in books and journals dealt with many female responsibilities, but, with a few exceptions, women's role in the transmission of Judaism and Jewish culture was conspicuously absent. The first, short-lived monthly periodical written expressly for women, *Di froyen-velt*, was published in New York in 1913. Calling itself in English "The Jewish Ladies Home Journal," it followed the typical formula of women's magazines of the time in providing columns on beauty, medical advice, cooking, and fashion along with romantic fiction.[52] However, it devoted several lead articles to defining the special problems confronting contemporary Jewish women, "who were the last to sense their inferior status in society [but] had accomplished in one generation what it took Gentile women generations to achieve with regard to emancipation."[53] In its second issue, in a powerful and lengthy article

51. Tashrak, *Etikete* (New York: Hebrew Publishing Co., 1912), pp. 43, 95, 156, 230.

52. *Di froyen-velt*, edited by A. Grayzel, was published in New York City from April through December 1913. It described itself as "a woman's journal dedicated to the Jewish home and family."

53. *Di froyen-velt* 1 (Apr. 1913): 4.

entitled "Our Daughters," the journal addressed itself, in terms reminiscent of public discourse in eastern Europe, to the dele-terious effect upon Jewish life in America of the failure to educate American-born daughters for their future responsi-bilities as Jewish wives and mothers. In addition to the general concerns she shared with all women, the Jewish woman had special duties as a Jewish mother: "She must see to it that her children, whose education lies in her hands, not be torn loose from our people. Into her hands is entrusted the fate of the future of our own history." The article doubted, however, that the American-born daughter, who was caught up with all the foolishness of the world, with "paint and powder" and junk novels, would be able to instill love of the Jewish people in her child or educate her child either as a responsible person (mentsh) or as a Jew. "We immigrants have made a mistake," continued the writer. "We thought that free education would solve all the problems of our children. We did not realize that we would have to work so hard that we would have to put our children into the factory as soon as we could. . . . They had no Jewish education but a factory education instead. Because of this mistake we have lost an entire generation, or even more." In conclusion, the writer called specifically for providing the immigrant daughter with "a healthy Jewish education," suffi-cient to withstand the effect of the workshop. It was necessary to give her "our national hopes" so that she would be proud of the fact that she was a child of the Jewish people.[54] At the end of the year Di froyen-velt provided an example to its female readers of how they, as mothers, could inculcate a positive sense of Jewishness in their children through the recount-ing of the Hanukkah story as part of the home celebration of

54. Ibid. 2 (May 1913): 3–5.

the holiday. Such an effort would subvert the shame that "our American children" felt about their Jewish roots and would inspire them to look differently at their parents and at themselves.[55]

The magazine celebrated the traditional value of domestic harmony (*sholom bayis*) but recognized the changed circumstances in which immigrant Jewish women and men lived. Reporting the difficult economic conditions of women both in the shop and at home, *Di froyen-velt* asserted that women, with their multiple responsibilities as supplemental breadwinners and household managers, experienced economic need more directly than did their husbands. Because of women's economic importance and as a result of the impact of modern ideas of equality and democracy, it was now clear that the biblical principle that "he will rule over her" could no longer serve as the fundamental basis of Jewish family life. The conditions of Jewish life in modern America called for an equal partnership of husband and wife within the home.[56]

Although American Orthodox spokesmen did not endorse the changes in Jewish family life and society that had been reinforced by mass migration, like their east European kin they recognized that the weakening of the structural supports of traditional Jewish life called into question the traditional practice of restricting the Jewish education of girls. As one newspaper reported in 1923:

55. "Hanukkah and Our Children," ibid., Dec. 1913, p. 3.

56. Article on *sholom bayis* in ibid., June 1913, p. 1; two articles on the economic situation of women in ibid., July 1913, p. 1, and Aug. 1913, p. 1. The biblical phrase "and he shall rule over you" (Genesis 3:16) was addressed by God to Eve as punishment for her disobedience and is cited as the justification for the subordination of women to men in both Jewish and Christian traditions.

This is a new anxiety, previously unknown to Judaism—an anxiety about the religious education of our women. . . . When the new times, with different biddings and different views, forced their ways into the [Jewish street], the women were the more defenseless in face of them; their examples were gone, and as for teaching, they had none to recall, the school had been closed to them, and now the household blessing was taken from them.[57]

However, this recognition of the need to provide Jewish religious education to girls to protect them from the lure of new American values apparently was not translated into concrete proposals for their instruction.

Chaim Malitz's 1918 book, Di heym un di froy (The home and the woman), is more typical in its concerns. Written with great respect for traditional Jewish values and with the stated purpose of encouraging marriage and family life, it exhorted the Jewish wife to be a baleboste (an efficient housewife). She was to keep her house clean and always be busy in order to make her husband, who slaved all day in factory or store, feel like a king at home.[58] Malitz expressed notions of a strict division of labor between husband and wife, separate spheres for each, and female moral superiority. He presented a sentimentalized view of the mother that reflected the bourgeois ideal. In his opinion, a wife enjoyed enormous powers of persuasion: "A wife can make of her husband all that she wants."[59] And a mother made the home: "Take away the mother from the

57. D. Kaufman, "How Shall We Raise the Religious Sense of Our Girls and Women?" Idishe likht 1 (4 May 1923): 10, as cited in Glanz, The Jewish Woman in America, 1:69.
58. Chaim Malitz, Di heym un di froy (New York: n.p., 1918), pp. 7, 15, 20–21, 45–47, 67.
59. Ibid., p. 14.

home, and there remains no home!"[60] But even he, while recognizing the importance of mothers in teaching their children to be honorable and good people, refrained from attributing to women any responsibility for their children's education as Jews, a subject he does not address at all.[61] And although he claimed that in Jewish families in America the general education of children had unfortunately been relegated entirely to the mother while the father's influence was entirely neglected, he blamed fathers, not mothers, for the situation.[62]

The monthly *Froyen zhurnal* (Ladies journal), published in 1922 and 1923 and aimed specifically at the growing number of middle-class immigrant women and their English-speaking daughters, provides a useful indication of how immigrant writers and editors viewed women's roles. The journal intended to bridge the gap between the generations, particularly by encouraging mothers and daughters together to select patterns for the latest fashions, lavishly illustrated in the pages of the magazine. Juxtaposing columns on cooking, child rearing, beauty, and sewing with romances, poetry, and news deemed of interest to women, it recognized and promoted the continued centrality of home and women's traditional roles while also praising women's expanded public roles.[63] Thus, an English-language article, entitled "Marriage Still Woman's Ideal," written by a woman and clearly designed for immigrant daughters, hailed the importance of women's

60. Ibid., p. 41. For the sentimentalization of the mother's role, see pp. 39–41.

61. Ibid., pp. 74, 76.

62. Ibid., pp. 58–62.

63. *Froyen zhurnal* (New York), Jan. 1922–Oct. 1923. For a brief discussion of the magazine, see Glanz, *The Jewish Woman in America*, 1:88, and Pratt, "Transitions in Judaism," pp. 691–92.

roles as wives and mothers: "The creation of a home is as specialized a field as any other. Here is the opportunity for women to take the initiative. It is their unique field. . . . Women of today have forgotten that there is a spiritual power in the material power that has been placed in their hands. They need to know how to combine the two."[64] Preserving the Jewish family's reputation for, as well as the reality of, domestic harmony was seen as primarily a woman's task. As Dr. Maurice Harris, in an article on the Jewish home, pointed out, "Israel, say our sages, was saved by the mothers. . . . Modern schools of Jewish thought may differ in their theology, but the ethical essentials of family life persist through all variations."[65]

The magazine included regular columns on Jewish holidays, on women in the Bible and Talmud, and on famous Jewish women in history, such as Grace Aguilar, Emma Lazarus, and Dorothea Mendelssohn. These articles appear to have been published for the purpose of edification of the readers, to convey to them that women had always been included in Jewish life, rather than to present explicit role models. Women's primary role was domestic, and they were expected to ensure the morality of the home, but the socialization of their children as Jews or the transmission of Jewish knowledge did not figure explicitly among their maternal responsibilities. Columns on child rearing were concerned with hygiene, not Torah.[66]

Yet this apolitical woman's journal clearly articulated that women's concern for home and family did not preclude their involvement in politics and civic affairs. The magazine in-

64. *Froyen zhurnal*, Aug. 1923, p. 50.
65. Ibid., Jan. 1923, p. 63.
66. Ibid., Jan. 1923, p. 39; Feb. 1923, p. 57; Mar. 1923, pp. 11, 17–18.

formed its readers how to become citizens and explained the nature of federal and state government to them, urging them to become familiar with the law so that they might be effective and responsible citizens. It assumed that its readers would want to be kept abreast of the activities of a variety of women's organizations, from the Women's International League for Peace and Freedom to the Zionist Women's League for Keren Hayessod. Among the advice columns about cooking, beauty, health, and etiquette were articles on how to found an organization and calls for women to organize their local benevolent societies on a national level.[67] The journal welcomed women's recent acquisition of suffrage. As one regular male contributor to the magazine wrote, "The events of these few brief years during which she has enjoyed this long overdue freedom amply justify the deed, as well as our most sanguine anticipations for the future years."[68]

Fully aware of the possibilities of combining social activism with the responsibilities of motherhood, some immigrant Jewish women organized themselves specifically to address the issue of raising children with a strong Jewish consciousness in the American environment, which was so uncongenial to the survival of ethnic consciousness. Mothers whose children attended afternoon classes at Yiddish supplementary schools in New York City established Sholom Aleichem Women's Clubs and held their first conference in March 1925.[69] Beginning with eight clubs founded with the assistance of teachers at the Harlem Sholom Aleichem Folk Shul, the net-

67. Ibid., Mar. 1923, pp. 8, 50.

68. Harold Berman, "Woman's Achievement," ibid., Jan. 1923, p. 66.

69. All information on this association comes from *Di idishe froy, Buletin aroysgegebn fun di Sholom Aleichem Froyen Klubn* 1, no. 1 (Nov. 1925).

work grew to sixteen, extended to Perth Amboy, New Jersey, and sent delegates to meetings of the Sholom Aleichem Folks Institute. The Sholom Aleichem clubs provided classes in Jewish history and literature to enable mothers to create a home environment supportive of the goals of the Yiddish schools. One article in the first bulletin of the Sholom Aleichem clubs, published in November 1925, announced in its title, "The home and the school must go hand in hand." Its author, Annie Newman, recognized that "it is a well established fact that with the best will the younger generation, even attending [Yiddish] school, will remain alien [fremd] to us when Jewish spirit is lacking in the Jewish home." Therefore, it was up to the clubs to assume the task of disseminating among women "the necessity of progressive national education. . . . The school must become secure with the assistance of [ideologically] conscious mothers.[70]

In fact, the lead article of the bulletin focused precisely on the relationship of the Jewish mother to the Jewish (Yiddish) school. Because in America the man is always "busy" (the word is cited in the Yiddish text in transliteration from the English) earning money, the mother was the only one to manage the home and educate the children. She was the only one who "could plant in the child a deep and true love of his people and awaken in him the self-consciousness and pride of . . . nationally oriented Jews. . . . The women united in the clubs assumed the task of developing themselves as Jewish women and of better understanding their task as mothers, in order to create a Jewish environment in the home that would help the school strengthen the progressive Jewish spirit in the child." Drawing upon the socialist concept of coopera-

70. Ibid., pp. 2, 3.

tive self-empowerment, the author noted that "the wives and mothers can join together in clubs and organizations and help one another in their spiritual development."[71]

Although the meaning of their Jewish identity differed from that of postemancipation Westernized Jewish women, who established women's philanthropic associations and assumed responsibility for instilling a moral and religious Jewish sensibility in their children, the women of the Sholom Aleichem clubs articulated a parallel maternal responsibility: the transmission to the younger generation of a secular nationalist and politically progressive Jewish identity. Both groups of women utilized their acceptance of gender differences in family life to expand the education of women as well as their domestic and social power and thereby to renegotiate the boundaries between private and public spheres.

Unlike such Yiddish-speaking immigrant women as the participants in the Sholom Aleichem clubs or such men as the writers for *Di froyen-velt*, who recognized in the immigrant period that the conditions of American life required that women take on the task of cultural transmission, American immigrant Jewish literature generally ignored the subject. Like most ethnic writers in America, immigrant and second-generation Jewish writers expressed profound ambivalence about their culture of origin or the culture of their parents, an ambivalence reflected in the theme of generational conflict so common in their fiction and memoirs.[72] Concerned with defining an appropriate American self, they focused on assimi-

71. Rokhl Muravchik, "The Jewish Mother and the Jewish School," ibid., p. 1.

72. Mary V. Dearborn, *Pocahontas's Daughters: Gender and Ethnicity in American Culture* (New York: Oxford University Press, 1986), p. 74.

lation rather than on cultural transmission, on east European Jewish tradition as a burden rather than a legacy. Yet the burden could not be cast off without doing psychological harm to the self. As Anzia Yezierska wrote of the tension between the desire for freedom and the need for connection: "I had to break away from my mother's cursing and my father's preaching to live my life; but without them I had no life. When you deny your parents, you deny the sky over your head. You become an outlaw, a pariah."[73] Mary Antin revealed less ambivalence in her autobiography, concluding confidently, "The past was only my cradle, and now it cannot hold me, because I am grown too big."[74] But in her life she suffered from disabling nervous disorders. Yezierska and Antin, the two most prominent Jewish women writers of the immigrant generation, both embraced assimilation as necessity and gift of liberation. They considered intermarriage with white American Protestants, a type of liaison that the literary critic Mary Dearborn has called "the Pocahontas union," the ultimate achievement of an American identity.[75] In her autobiography Antin alluded only obliquely to her marriage to a Christian professor at Columbia University in her reference to "an invitation to live in New York that I did not like to refuse"; Yezierska, on the other hand, wrote obsessively about interethnic romance, although most such relationships in her fiction failed, as, incidentally, did Antin's marriage.[76]

Women appear in the fiction and memoirs written by immigrants or their children primarily as mothers rather than as

73. Yezierska, *Red Ribbon on a White Horse*, p. 72, as cited in ibid., p. 77.
74. Mary Antin, *The Promised Land*, p. 364.
75. Dearborn, *Pocahontas's Daughters*, pp. 81, 104–5.
76. Antin, *The Promised Land*, p. 360.

the ambitious young girls seeking self-empowerment through education who were the primary heroines of Yezierska's stories and Antin's autobiography. Immigrant and second-generation writers celebrated immigrant Jewish mothers as the physical and psychological supporters of their families. The stereotypical image of the "Yiddishe Mamma" was a romanticized model of self-sacrifice for her children and a marvel of domestic wizardry. In his 1930 novel *The Mother*, Scholem Asch extolled his mother's miraculous feats as a provider living in poverty:

> They were wonderful, those cooking pots of mother's. . . . She gave them cold water—and the pots yielded yesterday's carrot soup anew; she gave them boiling water and the pots returned a royal dish. . . . Just one formula of extortion did mother possess for use on her pots—a sigh. When the pots heard mother sigh it was as though she had repeated a secret incantation over them, with which she adjured them to supply the pitifully meager bit of nourishment which was all she demanded for her large brood.[77]

The Yiddishe Mamma was also the emotional center of her family. Alfred Kazin offered a paradigmatic portrait of this facet of the immigrant mother's role in his memoir *A Walker in the City*:

> The kitchen gave a special character to our lives: my mother's character. All my memories of that kitchen are dominated by the nearness of my mother sitting all day long at her sewing machine. . . . Year by year, as I began to take in her fantastic capacity

77. Scholem Asch, *The Mother*, trans. Nathan Ausubel (New York: Liveright, 1930), pp. 8–9. The depiction of Sarah Rifke's magic pots refers to the mother in her Old Country setting, but this type of image also appears in the period of immigration.

for labor and her anxious zeal, I realized it was ourselves she kept stitched together.[78]

Although Kazin was writing nostalgically in the early 1950s, the Yiddishe Mamma had entered American popular culture in the 1920s through such vehicles as *The Jazz Singer* (in both stage and film versions) and Sophie Tucker's rendition of the song "My Yiddishe Mamma." This idealized representation of the immigrant Jewish mother as an undefeated source of strength was qualified by other early literary portraits. Sometimes her children sympathetically presented the immigrant mother as a victim of grinding poverty in the slums or of the patriarchal authority enshrined in traditional Judaism. Michael Gold, for example, in his autobiographical novel *Jews without Money*, lamented the suffering of his hardworking mother, Katie, who "slaved, worked herself to the bone keeping us fresh and neat." When her husband became disabled in an accident at work, at a time when there was no workmen's compensation, she worked at a cafeteria from early in the morning until five-thirty, when she returned home to make supper and clean the house. For this communist writer, his pious Jewish mother, the instigator of a rent strike, becomes the symbol of the sins of capitalism and the inspiration for his commitment to social justice and compassion for the poor. Yet he proudly depicted his mother in terms far from those of contemporary descriptions of the lady: "How can I ever forget this dark little woman with bright eyes, who hobbled about all day in bare feet, cursing in Elizabethan Yiddish, using the forbidden words 'ladies' do not use, smacking us, beating us, fighting with her neighbors, helping

78. Alfred Kazin, *A Walker in the City* (New York: Harcourt, Brace, 1951), pp. 66–67.

her neighbors, busy from morn to midnight in the tenement struggle for life."[79]

In Bread Givers, her best-known novel, Anzia Yezierska portrayed a mother so subordinated by the personality and male privilege of her tyrannical Talmud scholar husband that she was unable to serve as a model for any of her daughters. Nor was she able to prevent the bartering of two of them in marriages that were to their father's financial advantage. Yet Sara Smolinsky acknowledges both her mother's unrelenting efforts to sustain her family and especially the love she gave so freely to her self-centered daughter. As she witnesses her mother's death, Sara describes "the love-light of Mother's eyes flow[ing] into mine" and feels "literally Mother's soul enter my soul like a miracle."[80] In her short stories Yezierska also wrote of the economic travail of strong but coarse immigrant Jewish mothers and of the bitterness of acculturation and economic success that estranged mothers from their children. Hannah Breineh in "The Fat of the Land" is a tough woman, whose love and concern for her brood are expressed in loud cursing, fierce bargaining with peddlers to save a penny or two, and domineering control of her children. Through her entrepreneurial skills she begins a process of social mobility that culminates in prosperity and resettlement of the family on Manhattan's Riverside Drive. Yet Hannah Breineh remains unacculturated and realizes in her old age that she is at home nowhere, neither on the Lower East Side, whose poverty and

79. Michael Gold, Jews without Money (New York: Horace Liveright, 1930; reprint, New York: Avon Books, 1965). The first quotation is from p. 48, the second is from p. 112, and the description of his mother's workday when employed is from p. 177.

80. Yezierska, Bread Givers, p. 252.

dirt repel her, nor on the Upper West Side, where she daily confronts the contempt of her children and the absence of friends who might understand her culture and experience.[81] In writing about the working-class immigrant mother, Gold and Yezierska refrained from romanticization but presented at least partly sympathetic portrayals of women caught in social circumstances over which they exercised no control, despite their personal strengths. With the movement of many immigrant Jewish families into the middle class in the interwar period, the suffering Jewish mother who managed to prepare her children for life in an America to which she remained a stranger was joined in American Jewish literature by women who symbolized the dark side of Americanization. Thus, leftist writers focused on women as representatives of capitalist excess. Along with his revered mother and the pathetic prostitutes who were his neighbors, Gold includes in his *Jews without Money* the ludicrous vision of an idle Jewish woman with money, the wife of his father's boss:

> Mrs. Cohen, a fat, middle-aged woman, lay on a sofa. She glittered like an ice cream parlor. Her tubby legs rested on a red pillow. Her bleached yellow head blazed with diamond combs and rested on a pillow of green. She wore a purple silk waist hung with yards of tapestry and lace. Diamonds shone from her ears; diamond rings sparkled from every finger. She looked like some vulgar, pretentious prostitute, but was only the typical wife of a Jewish *nouveau riche*.[82]

81. Yezierska, "The Fat of the Land," in *Hungry Hearts* (Boston and New York: Houghton-Mifflin, 1920); reprinted in *The Open Cage: An Anzia Yezierska Collection*, selected and with an introduction by Alice Kessler-Harris (New York: Persea Books, 1979), pp. 77–104.

82. Gold, *Jews without Money*, p. 156.

Gold does not portray her husband, Zechariah, the owner of a house-painting business and a dabbler in real estate, as an object of derision, even though the boss visits only once after the father's accident and provides no assistance to the family. Similarly, Clifford Odets represented the middle-class immigrant Jewish mother as a symbol of bourgeois values that suppressed idealism in the name of ambition and material success.[83]

Despite the multiplicity of representations of the immigrant Jewish mother, the sentimental image of the Yiddishe Mamma endured, perhaps because she served as a useful foil to the far more negative stereotypes of the second- and third-generation American Jewish woman that were to emerge largely after the Second World War. Memoirs and recent studies based upon oral histories also recall the immigrant mother in images that resemble the Yiddishe Mamma, though in less idealized terms.[84] Looking back, the children of immigrants express appreciation for their mothers' efforts to sustain their families amid poverty and squalor. Although their home experiences differ, most see their mothers as mediators between the home and the larger society of school, work, and recreation even if, because their style was foreign, they could

83. See, e.g., Clifford Odets, *Awake and Sing!* (New York: Random House, 1935). For a brief analysis of the changing image of the Jewish mother in American Jewish literature, see Beverly Gray Bienstock, "The Changing Image of the American Jewish Mother," in *Changing Images of the Family*, ed. Virginia Tufte and Barbara Myerhoff (New Haven: Yale University Press, 1979), pp. 173–91.

84. For the use of oral history testimony to reclaim the experiences of immigrant women and their children, see Weinberg, *The World of Our Mothers*.

not serve as explicit role models for adult life in America. Far from being rigidly conservative in their views of their children's behavior, mothers are remembered, at least by their daughters, as being generally supportive of their children's aspirations and desires for independence and education. Indeed, despite Sophie Tucker's role in the popularization of the term, the sentimentalized Yiddishe Mamma seems to have been a creation of her sons.[85]

Perhaps immigrant mothers could be more flexible regarding their children's self-assertion because the experience of migration was less traumatic for them than for their husbands.[86] As in the case of the middle-class Jewish women of western and central Europe and America, their primary role within the family rather than the workplace shielded them from immediate demands to abandon traditional Jewish practice to earn a living and achieve social mobility. The female ideal of the *baleboste* also differed little from Pinsk to the Lower East Side. Because of her acknowledged centrality in the home, the immigrant Jewish woman may have suffered less loss of self-esteem than her husband, who, initially at least, eked out a living in the far from prestigious occupations of tailor or peddler. Moreover, one element of social status avail-

85. Ibid., pp. 122–23, 241. Beverly Bienstock points out that the mother in *The Jazz Singer* is "less a preserver of the old ways than a mediator between two conflicting systems of values." See Bienstock, "The Changing Image of the American Jewish Mother," pp. 171–77; the quotation is from p. 177.

86. Irving Howe has argued that the "disarranged family structure" of Jewish immigrants, caused by the father's traumatic experience, gave the Jewish mother "powers she had never known before" (*World of Our Fathers*, p. 177).

able to men within eastern European Jewish society—mastery of rabbinic texts—did not survive the overseas migration.[87] Although immigrant mothers and fathers both experienced conflict with their Americanized children, who often viewed them with embarrassment,[88] the maternal caretaking role may have preserved affective ties in the home between mothers and their grown offspring.

The immigrant generation had two major concerns: economic survival in the new land and accommodation to the norms of American life. As they strove to achieve the twin goals of economic security and Americanization, Jewish women and men saw their roles as different but complementary. All Jews—whether philanthropists and social reformers of the already established American Jewish community or the immigrants themselves—recognized acculturation as a necessity for immigrants to achieve a stable position in America. In the context of the immigrant experience, as in the east European Jewish community, the process of assimilation did not yet exceed the goals of the Jewish leaders who articulated the project of assimilation. To be sure, just as Jewish spokesmen in eastern Europe were reflecting on the deleterious consequences of the more rapid secularization of Jewish girls than boys, leaders of the New York City Kehillah, like Judah Magnes, Samson Benderly, Alexander Dushkin, Isaac Berkson, Israel Friedlaender, and Mordecai Kaplan, were promoting

87. On the impact of this change in sources of status, see most notably Abraham Cahan, *The Rise of David Levinsky* (New York: Harper & Brothers, 1917).

88. Howe, *World of Our Fathers*, pp. 261–63; on children's discomfort with their parents' speaking Yiddish in public, see Metzker, ed., *A Bintel Brief*, pp. 156–58.

Jewish education for both sexes because of their concern for the increasing alienation of the children of the immigrants from Jewish tradition and culture.[89] By innovating in the area of education for girls, they introduced a change in prescribed gender roles in their project of assimilation. Yet, as we have seen, in the first immigrant generation in America, Jewish education for children of either sex was low on the parental agenda. Because of the availability of free public schooling, which was the primary instrument of Americanization and open to girls as well as boys, the issue of gender in the process of assimilation attracted scant attention.

With the emergence of second-generation Jews as a prominent force within American Jewry in the 1920s,[90] the American Jewish community, as chapter 1 indicated, adopted the understanding of gender roles that characterized middle-class Jews in all the countries of the industrialized West. The *baleboste* gave way to the Jewish priestess in her home, and in the course of time the Yiddishe Mamma of song and story was transmuted into Sophie Portnoy.

89. On the educational work of the Kehillah, see Arthur A. Goren, *New York Jews and the Quest for Community: The Kehillah Experiment, 1908–1922* (New York: Columbia University Press, 1970), pp. 86–133. On Israel Friedlaender's involvement, see Bella Round Shargel, *Practical Dreamer: Israel Friedlaender and the Shaping of American Judaism* (New York: Jewish Theological Seminary, 1985), pp. 125–29.

90. For the by now classic work on this subject, see Deborah Dash Moore, *At Home in America: Second Generation New York Jews* (New York: Columbia University Press, 1981).

# 4

# The Sexual Politics of Jewish Identity

"Women are, in a certain sense, like the Jewish people."[1] So wrote the New York immigrant journalist Chaim Malitz in his 1918 book Di heym un di froy in a section that described the lack of recognition that women receive for their work. Jews, too, he noted, failed to gain respect in the world. Whereas Malitz suggested that women were like Jews, many Gentile observers of Jewish life in the late nineteenth and early twentieth centuries depicted male Jews in terms more often ascribed to women. Particularly in the societies of the industrialized West, Jewish men, even though they had assimilated to Western culture, were seen as unmanly. As the historian Joan Wallach Scott reminds us, gender is not merely about the socially and culturally defined differences between the sexes. It is also "a primary way of signifying relationships of power."[2] By caricaturing Jewish men as feminized, antisemites and their fellow travelers attempted to strip them of the power and honor otherwise due them as men, especially as economically successful men. Jewish men, in turn, as they experienced emancipation and the conditions of middle-class life and anticipated the rewards of both, responded to their disparagement in cultures influenced by antisemitism by creating negative representations of Jewish women. Struggling to gain respect and power for themselves as men in a far from open larger society, male Jews defined an identity that not only distin-

1. Malitz, Di heym un di froy, p. 80.
2. Scott, Gender and the Politics of History, p. 42.

guished them from women but also displaced their own anxieties upon women. Just as Jews remained the primal Other in secular cultures still marked by Christian prejudices, so did women in Jewish culture. Jewish men, first in the countries of western and central Europe and later in America, constructed a modern Jewish identity that devalued women, the Other within the Jewish community. Although the terms of opprobrium varied with time and setting, as the social and cultural position of Jewish men and women changed in different societies, the focus on gender as essential in the construction of Jewish identity and in the project of assimilation strikes me as a key component, though obviously not the only one, in interpreting Jewish self-definition in the modern period.[3]

The sexual politics of Jewish identity at the turn of the twentieth century, when issues of gender came to the fore, is closely linked to the heightening of antisemitism and to Jewish responses to the phenomenon. The focus on gender provides a new perspective on antisemitic claims and their impact on the project of assimilation. In examining the

3. Although I include in this chapter material drawn from the European Zionist movement, I have chosen not to investigate issues of gender in the Zionist settlement in Palestine or in modern Hebrew literature. For an introduction to gender issues in the Zionist experience, see Biale, *Eros and the Jews*, pp. 176–203. For a discussion of the experience of women pioneers in Palestine and their efforts to define and achieve equality, see Deborah Bernstein, *The Struggle for Equality: Urban Women Workers in Pre-state Israeli Society* (New York: Praeger Publications, 1987), and her edited volume *Pioneers and Homemakers: Jewish Women in Pre-state Israel* (Albany: State University of New York Press, 1992), as well as the collection of sources found in Rachel Katznelson Shazar, ed., *The Plough Woman: Memoirs of the Pioneer Women of Palestine*, trans. Maurice Samuel (1932; reprint, New York: Herzl Press, 1975).

formation of modern Jewish identity, it is useful to focus upon those who articulated most strongly the perniciousness of Jewish traits and the consequent unacceptability of Jews within society. I shall therefore pay particular attention to European antisemites and to those Jews who internalized their message, whom we label "self-hating Jews."[4] Of course, most Europeans were not virulent antisemites nor were most Jews self-loathing. However, extremists often point to social and psychological tensions that others feel or express in more-muted terms. Since even those who supported civil rights for Jews saw them as being in need of, and capable of, improvement and viewed Judaism largely with contempt, it is fair to state that prevailing cultural attitudes toward Jews in the very societies they were eager to join were generally disparaging. Indeed, those attitudes became more negative at the end of the century that followed the first emancipation of the Jews as the racism of the extremists changed the terms of debate that had been set during the Enlightenment by asserting the futility of hopes for Jewish self-improvement. Antisemites and self-hating Jews thus suggest the essential conflict in men's shaping of their Jewish identity.

In the last decades of the nineteenth century antisemitism acquired a political dimension in western and central Europe that baffled Jews of the time. They had optimistically assumed that history moved only in the direction of an enlightened

4. The phenomenon was first studied in a scholarly fashion by a German Jew, Theodor Lessing, in his Der jüdischer Selbsthass (1930; reprint, Munich: Mattes & Seitz Verlag, 1984). See also Kurt Lewin, "Self-Hatred among Jews," written in 1941, in Resolving Social Conflicts, ed. Gertrud Weiss Lewin (New York: Harper & Brothers, 1948), pp. 186–200. For the latest study, see Sander L. Gilman, Jewish Self-Hatred: Anti-Semitism and the Hidden Language of the Jews (Baltimore: Johns Hopkins University Press, 1986).

progress. Moreover, the development of a political ideology of antisemitism reinforced and legitimated social and cultural manifestations of antisemitism that had never been fully eradicated by Enlightenment rationalism. Ironically, the very generation of Jews who had acquired the financial resources, education, and manners of the bourgeoisie did not achieve the social status and psychological well-being associated with their class. Instead, they were compelled to refashion their identities in response to endemic antisemitism—an antisemitism that was also misogynist. This coincidence of antisemitism and misogyny is understandable, for in disputing their subordination and asserting a claim to equality, both modern Jews and modern women challenged the antisemites' nostalgic and antimodern vision of a smoothly functioning, non-egalitarian, hierarchical social order, in which subordinate groups (like women and Jews) knew their place.[5]

The target of antisemitic bile was the male Jew, so visible because of his brilliantly successful participation in the economy and culture of the larger society. Increasingly, he was depicted as "womanish." Like women, Jewish men were seen as weak, as soft and rounded.[6] Continued obsession on the part of such central European intellectuals as Arthur Schopenhauer with the "Jewish odor" undermined the heterosexual gender identity of male Jews by drawing an analogy between them and

5. For a discussion of this confluence, see Shulamit Volkov, "Antisemitism as a Cultural Code—Reflections on the History and Historiography of Antisemitism in Imperial Germany," *Leo Baeck Institute Yearbook* 23 (1978): 31–35.

6. George Mosse describes the antisemitic stereotype of the Jewish male in the following terms: "a contorted figure resting on short legs, a greedy and sensual corpulence" (*The Crisis of German Ideology: Intellectual Origins of the Third Reich* [New York: Grosset & Dunlap, 1964], p. 140).

menstruating females.[7] Moreover, the growing interest in eugenics in both Europe and the United States and the conviction of the centrality of a genetically strong stock for national success drew attention to the supposed racial deterioration of the Jews. In Europe the fashionable concepts of degeneracy and decadence, ironically popularized by a Jewish writer, Max Nordau, among others, fueled the fire.[8] In America the fear that the country was being overrun and weakened by immigrants of inferior genetic quality prompted pseudoscientific comment designed to encourage immigrant restriction. In both milieus the Jewish male was depicted as physically weak, incapable of the hard labor required of productive citizens.[9] As one 1903 article published in America asserted, "Jewish immigrants of a military age who could pass our army requirements for recruits are comparatively rare."[10]

As for their characters, Jewish men were represented as ma-

7. Jay Geller, "(G)nos(e)ology: The Cultural Construction of the Other," in People of the Body: Jews and Judaism from an Embodied Perspective, ed. Howard Eilberg-Schwartz (Albany: State University of New York Press, 1992), pp. 250–53.

8. See Max Nordau, Degeneration, trans. from the 2d ed. of the German work (New York: D. Appleton, 1895). On Nordau, see Meir Ben-Horin, Max Nordau, Philosopher of Human Solidarity (New York: Conference on Jewish Social Studies, 1956), and George Mosse, "Max Nordau, Liberalism and the New Jew," Journal of Contemporary History 27, no. 4 (Oct. 1992): 565–81.

9. Sander L. Gilman, The Jew's Body (New York and London: Routledge, 1991), esp. pp. 52–53.

10. Roger Mitchell, "Recent Jewish Immigration to the United States," Popular Science Monthly, Feb. 1903, p. 342, as cited in Robert Singerman, "The Jew as Racial Alien: The Genetic Component of American Anti-Semitism," in Anti-Semitism in American History, ed. David A. Gerber (Urbana and Chicago: University of Illinois Press, 1986), p. 109.

terialistic, manipulative, and lacking in moral vigor and honor. That is, they shared with women a behavioral style found among the socially powerless. In his study *Jewish Self-Hatred: Anti-Semitism and the Hidden Language of the Jews*, Sander Gilman adds to the parallels drawn between Jews and women their supposed false and manipulative use of language, their faulty logic, and their substitution of mockery and satire for true humor.[11] In the German-speaking countries, even assimilated Jews were depicted as unable to use German properly; their language remained encoded with Yiddish inflections and intonations. Similarly, in the antisemitic caricatures that proliferated in France at the time of the Dreyfus Affair, the speech of Jews was transcribed bearing a heavy Yiddish or Germanic accent.[12] Although the caricature of the Jew who could not speak correctly had already appeared in England during the conflict about the "Jew bill" of 1753, the survival of the stereotyped image into the late nineteenth century, when Jews in the West, with the exception of recent immigrants, spoke without accents, suggests its power to diminish the masculine authority of Jewish males. Finally, in analyzing the theme of a joke included in an early-nineteenth-century German collection of Jewish jokes, Gilman notes that this joke reflects the prevailing sentiment that "Jews, when oppressed, can attack only verbally. In this they are like women, whose lack of strength is compensated for by their wit."[13]

Even sophisticated interpreters of human behavior could

11. Gilman, *Jewish Self-Hatred*, pp. 243–45, 267.

12. For examples of these caricatures, see Kleeblatt, ed., *The Dreyfus Affair*, pp. 77, 91, 161, 184.

13. Gilman, *Jewish Self-Hatred*, p. 258.

read the nonviolent reactions of Jewish men to the demeaning acts or speech of antisemites as "unmanly." After all, Sigmund Freud himself reacted with a sense of shame to a story told him in his childhood by his father, Jacob—a story that became one of his central childhood memories. Jacob Freud recounted that many years before in their hometown of Freiburg, Moravia, he had had an encounter on the street with a non-Jew, who knocked his new fur cap from his head and shouted at him to get off the sidewalk. "And what did you do?" asked the young Sigmund. "I stepped into the road and picked up my cap," Jacob replied. That response, Freud recalled, "did not seem heroic to me . . . from a big strong man."[14] The Jewish father was found wanting as a model of masculinity by his famous son, who based his theories of healthy male psychological development upon the resolution of the Oedipal conflict of son and father.

Male immigrant Jewish members of the working class, too, lacking both the refined manners and the sedentary intellectual jobs held by so many middle- and upper-class Jewish men in western and central Europe and the United States, were perceived by contemporary observers as deficient in masculine characteristics. The historian David Feldman has found contempt for male Jewish workers in English attitudes toward London's East End immigrant Jews at the turn of the century. British trade unionists attributed their lack of success in establishing firmly rooted unions among immigrant Jews to "their want of manly virtues." Similarly a London policeman of the time, commenting upon the orderly conduct of poor Jewish

14. For an account of Freud's reaction to his father's tale, see Gay, Freud, pp. 11–12.

immigrants, dismissed their good behavior with the remark that "the Jews are not men enough to be rough." [15]

If Jewish men were widely perceived to lack the physical strength and bravado that characterized others of their sex, in fin de siècle Europe they were also deemed, particularly by physician-psychologists, to resemble women in yet another way: they shared the female tendency to a type of nervous disorder, hysteria. In another study, The Jew's Body, Gilman points out that male Jews, in becoming the prototype for the hysteric, were once again feminized: "For if the visual representation of the hysteric within the world of images of the nineteenth century was the image of the female, its subtext was that feminized males, such as Jews, were also hysterics. . . . [T]he face of the Jew became the face of the hysteric." [16]

The association of stereotypic female traits with male Jewishness appears explicitly and with great clarity in the writings of German and Austrian antisemites, who were, virtually without exception, misogynist as well as antisemitic. The German youth movement, which was permeated with antisemitic attitudes, not only contrasted Aryan male beauty with Jewish ugliness but also excluded women from membership since only men were fit to lead the Volk (the people). At German and Austrian universities, fraternities and other student groups, permeated with volkisch ideology, likewise barred Jews from membership. Jews then established their own student associations, which engaged in many of the pursuits promoted by the fraternities, such as the sport of dueling. In refusing to ac-

15. David Feldman, Englishmen and Jews: Social Relations and Political Culture, 1840–1914 (New Haven: Yale University Press, 1994), p. 285.

16. Gilman, The Jew's Body, p. 63.

cept Jews as worthy opponents in the duels that established masculine prowess, German and Austrian youth treated male Jews as though they were women. In the eyes of their fellow students, Jews, even when organized in their own groups, continued to lack honor.[17]

Within the Jewish community, Zionists took the lead in combating the antisemitic depiction of the male Jew by presenting a counterimage, the "New Jew," who was the mirror opposite of the antisemitic stereotype of the Jew. If the Diaspora Jew was physically weak and soft, the Zionist New Jew was strong and muscular. If the Diaspora Jew signaled the physical and moral degeneration of the Jewish people, the Zionist New Jew represented its physical and spiritual rebirth. If the Diaspora Jew was manipulative and wily, the Zionist New Jew was straightforward and direct. If the Diaspora Jew was a huckster or middleman, the Zionist New Jew was a peasant farmer or an efficient technocrat. Not only did the Zionists reject the Diaspora societies that treated Jews as eternal aliens, no matter how complete their assimilation, but in seeking to create the New Jew, they also rejected the modern West's equation of Jewishness with femininity, for the New Jew was clearly and unabashedly a masculine creature.

The initial promoters of this new model for healthy Jewish identity were Zionist figures educated in the increasingly antisemitic societies of central Europe. Both Theodor Herzl, the charismatic leader of political Zionism, and Max Nordau, the prominent intellectual and popular writer who was his close associate in the early years of the Zionist movement,

17. On the barring of Jews from fraternities beginning in 1878, see Mosse, *The Crisis of German Ideology*, p. 135. On the male ideal of the youth movement, see pp. 176–77.

shared the antisemites' assessment of the social characteristics of Diaspora Jewry. However, they saw in Zionism the possibility for a fundamental transformation of those characteristics through the physical and spiritual redemption of the Jews.

In his 1902 utopian novel, *Altneuland* (Old new land), Theodor Herzl depicted a flourishing Zionist society in the future Palestine of 1923.[18] That society was populated by Jews who were the antithesis of the materialistic, social-climbing, ugly Jews of the urban centers of central and western Europe, the stereotypic Jews of European literature and art at the turn of the century.[19] Indeed, the effect of Diaspora life on the hero of the tale, a Viennese lawyer named Friedrich Loewenberg who has chosen to leave Europe to live cut off from society on a tropical island, is described years later by his noble Prussian companion: "Well our island did not disagree with you, Fritz. What a green, hollow-chested Jewboy you were when I took you away."[20] Herzl's Palestinian Jews were, in contrast, suntanned technologically sophisticated builders of a prosperous new society. Proud of their accomplishments, they had no need to indulge themselves with needless luxury. Although women possessed political equality in Herzl's Zionist society and are commended for having "worked faithfully" beside the men in the period of reconstruction, they choose to devote themselves to their domestic responsibilities in place of civic

18. Theodor Herzl, *Old-New Land* ("*Altneuland*"), trans. Lotta Levenson (1941; reprint, New York: Markus Wiener Publishing and Herzl Press, 1987).

19. For the visual stereotype of the Jewish bourgeoisie in fin de siècle Europe, see Kleeblatt, ed., *The Dreyfus Affair*, pp. 77, 81–82.

20. Herzl, *Old-New Land*, p. 54.

participation. As a "sensible society," however, Zionist Palestine recruits young women as well as young men for two years of social service and uses "old maids, the single women who were sneered at or looked upon as a burden," to conduct public charities.[21]

Max Nordau was even more influential than Herzl in creating and disseminating the ideal of the New Jew. In response to antisemitic critiques of Jewish weakness, he popularized the term "muskeljudentum" ("muscular Judaism" or "muscular Jewry"), initially in a brief article that he published in 1900 in the Jüdische Turnzeitung (Jewish gymnastics newspaper) and in subsequent speeches and writing.[22] For Nordau, only through conscious effort could the Jew achieve the physical strength that characterized healthy men. Calling upon his audience to take his message to heart, he wrote, "Let us once more become deep-chested, taut-limbed, bold-eyed men."[23] As he proclaimed the following year in an address to the Fifth Zionist Congress entitled "The Moral and Physical Recovery of the Jews," "[F]or a number of Jews, even the most proud, it is an obvious fact that the Jew is clumsy and lamentably awkward in physical terms; that he is characterized by a pitiable weakness."[24] His concept of "muscular Jewry" was designed

21. Ibid., pp. 75, 77.

22. Max Nordau, "Muskeljudentum," Jüdische Turnzeitung, June 1900; reprinted in his Zionistische Schriften (Cologne and Leipzig: Jüdischer Verlag, 1909), pp. 379–81. See also Biale, Eros and the Jews, pp. 177–79.

23. Zionistische Schriften, p. 380.

24. Max Nordau, "Relèvement moral et physique des Juifs: Discours au 5e Congrès sioniste," L'écho sioniste, 15 Jan. 1902; reprinted in his Ecrits sionistes, ed. Baruch Hagani (Paris: Librairie Lipschutz, 1936), p. 112. See also his "Was bedeutet das Turnen für uns Juden," Jüdische Turnzeitung, July 1902; reprinted in his Zionistische Schriften, pp. 382–88.

to counter these unfortunate consequences of Diaspora conditions. To realize Nordau's goals, the Zionist movement from its earliest years sponsored sports and gymnastics clubs to remake Jewish bodies along with Jewish minds. The historian Michael Berkowitz has concluded in his study of the creation of a Zionist national culture for central and western European Jews that these athletic associations "constituted a significant means of displaying a new Jewish male type. . . . Exhibitions of the [gymnastic clubs], ostensible signs of Zionism's manliness, strength, and vigor, became a greatly anticipated and prideful aspect of the festivities which complemented the [Zionist] Congresses' proceedings."[25]

Muscular Jewry also made its appearance in the visual representations of Zionism. When the early Zionist movement created official commemorative postcards of the congresses that portrayed the Jewish future in Palestine, it presented scenes of young and vigorous males engaged in agricultural labor. Although female figures occasionally appeared in the postcards, they did so primarily in symbolic form, as the representation of Zionism and the happy future it portended for the Jewish people. The use of Theodor Herzl's photographic portrait was also designed to disseminate a positive male image of the Jew.[26] In fact, the publicists of the Zionist movement promoted male solidarity as an essential precondition for nation building. Like other nationalist movements of the time, Zionism presupposed a linkage between masculinity and civic consciousness. Male activists were responsible

25. Michael Berkowitz, Zionist Culture and West European Jewry, p. 99. For his discussion of Nordau and the importance of Zionist athletics, see pp. 107–9.

26. Ibid., pp. 120–24, 135–38.

for the direction of the nation, and full participation in the public life of the nation was limited to men alone.[27]

Although Zionism in theory promised equality between the sexes, when European Zionist intellectuals and activists wrote specifically about women's role in the national movement, they fell back upon the bourgeois ideal of separate spheres with its assumption of the naturalness of gender divisions. Although they dissented strongly from the project of assimilation, they expressed sentiments about women's historic role as sustainer of the Jewish family that could have been endorsed by anti-Zionist Jewish communal leaders. In 1917 and 1918 two pamphlets on women targeting a female audience were published under Zionist auspices.[28] Both appealed to women to join the Zionist cause and proclaimed that women had an important role to play in the movement. That role, however, was limited to their functions as wives and mothers.

As intellectual and spiritual leader of German-speaking Zionism, Martin Buber called upon Jewish women to contribute to the spiritual rebirth of the Jewish people by re-

27. Ibid., pp. 18–19, 92–94; George Mosse, *Nationalism and Sexuality: Respectability and Abnormal Sexuality in Modern Europe* (New York: Howard Fertig, 1985), pp. 17, 112. On Zionist women's struggle for equality, consult the sources listed in n. 3 above.

28. They were *Di yudishe froy un der Tsionizm* (Warsaw: Druckerei "Hazefira," 1918) and Nahum Sokolow, *Idishe froy* (London: English Zionist Federation, 1917). Although both were published in Yiddish, the first, which included articles by Martin Buber, Sara Pomerantz, and Marta Baer-Issachar, was clearly written originally for a western, rather than an eastern, European readership (since readers are exhorted on pp. 25–26 to understand the needs of their brethren in the east and to learn from them). Biale (*Eros and the Jews*, p. 182) mentions what is clearly a German version of Buber's essay, published in 1920.

claiming their traditional role within the family. Celebrating her strength in the ghetto, Buber praised the Jewish woman for concentrating her life on her family, thereby enabling her husband to develop his spiritual and intellectual interests, and raising their children as steadfast Jews.[29] With emancipation, however, Jewish women had abandoned their traditional role and had thrown themselves into assimilation, with the result that the Jewish family was destroyed, Jewish solidarity eliminated, and independent Jewish culture eradicated. The Jewish woman had become alienated from her own circles, and "where she was once the sovereign in her own house, now she was the slave of her Christian maid."[30] Although she bore considerable guilt for the decline of the Jewish people, the Jewish woman had an even greater part to play in their rebirth. By returning to the home and developing her own sense of Jewishness, her love of her people, she had the capacity, based on her natural intuition and activity, to become a queen once more, to restore Jewish family life to its former glory and to instill in her children pride in their origins, and even in their physical appearance, as Jews. Buber concluded by noting that "although only men could invent and justify culture-ideas, they could not create fully realized, living-effective culture without women."[31]

29. Martin Buber, "Dos Tsiyon fun der yudisher froy," in Di yudishe froy un der Tsionizm, p. 6.

30. Ibid., p. 8. This phrase must have enjoyed wide currency in Zionist circles, since Sokolow had made precisely the same statement the previous year, though couched in the second, rather than the third, person. See Sokolow, Idishe froy, p. 20.

31. Buber, "Dos Tsiyon fun der yudisher froy," pp. 8–10. The quotation is from p. 10.

Sara Pomerantz and Marta Baer-Issachar expressed variations on Buber's themes, prescribing women's roles solely in terms of their domestic responsibilities and criticizing the involvement of Jewish women in the public, universalist causes of the day rather than concentrating on the aspirations and suffering of their own people. Pomerantz deplored the fact that Jewish women had been increasingly attracted to all that was foreign, even though the larger society, both in the street and in the salon, responded with antisemitism. In raising their children without a Jewish national consciousness, Jewish mothers failed to prepare them for the world in which they would live. It was the Jewish mother's task, she concluded, to "give back the nation to her child" and through Zionism provide him with a high ideal.[32] Baer-Issachar noted that Jewish women's enthusiasm for the issue of women's rights had contributed to their growing distance from their people. Excusing the women of her own time, she laid the blame for Jewish women's alienation upon the prior generation. Addressing those Jewish women who still stood aside from serving their people's cause, she appealed to their desire to participate in the heroic and inspirational task of bringing rescue and hope to their people. Using feminist rhetoric to divert Jewish women from the feminist cause, she called upon them to make themselves strong so that the Jewish people could give the world "the new woman . . . who sees her future in not renouncing her femininity and who happily believes that she should not be involved in men's work but only in that which will make our people healthy. . . . She struggles

32. Pomerantz, "Di tsionistishe ide'e un di yudishe froy," in *Di yudishe froy un der Tsionizm*, pp. 13–19. The quotation is from p. 18.

not for women's rights but she seeks . . . women's duties."[33] Those duties, although social tasks, were dictated by nature, as they were among every people, and were subsumed in responsibilities for house and family, particularly in the education of one's children, which necessitated the education of women.[34] Yet the needs of the people and of the Zionist cause led Baer-Issachar to expand women's domestic role to include fund-raising for the building of the motherland.[35]

Surveying the important role that Jewish women had played from biblical times in the defense of the Jewish people, Nahum Sokolow pointed out to his female readers, whom he addressed throughout in the second person, that Jewish women, as mothers, had always strengthened the people by creating the Jewish home: "You made family life like a dear, antique embroidery. . . . A locked, folksy, pure . . . temple was the Jewish home."[36] The assimilation that followed upon emancipation, however, was a deadly poison for Jewish women; they lost both respect and self-respect along with the iron moral discipline of Jewish family life. Yet their efforts at assimilation were doomed to failure because their style and character were, like it or not, connected through their blood to their grandmothers and great-grandmothers, not to the alien peoples of Europe with whom they desired to integrate.[37] Like the other Zionist publicists, Sokolow called

33. Baer-Issachar, "Tsu unzere froyen," in ibid., pp. 20–24. The quotation is from pp. 23–24.

34. Ibid., pp. 25–27. Baer-Issachar also included sports and gymnastics in women's self-education.

35. Ibid., pp. 28–30.

36. Sokolow, Idishe froy, pp. 3–13. The quotation is from p. 12.

37. Ibid., pp. 19–20.

upon women to dedicate themselves, along with men, to the Jewish people's task of self-liberation and concluded his pamphlet with a ringing question: "will you come back to your house, O Jewish woman?"[38]

Most Western Jews, however, did not resolve their questions about their identity and status by becoming Zionists. Indeed, Zionism did not "capture the communities" of the Diaspora until after the establishment of the State of Israel. While Zionists directly countered the antisemitic caricature of the male Jew as a feminized creature through the creation of the New Jew, the majority of Jewish men living in Western societies constructed their identities through a more oblique version of sexual politics.

Some highly assimilated Jews internalized the dominant society's antisemitic representation of Jewishness and projected their own hatred of Jewish characteristics on other individual Jews, on other groups of Jews (such as east Europeans), or on themselves.[39] Perhaps the most influential and reflective of these self-hating Jews were the young Austrian philosopher Otto Weininger and the successful German industrialist, intellectual, and statesman Walther Rathenau. Both of them addressed the Jewish question with great concern, Rathenau in the 1897 essay "Hear, O Israel" and Weininger in his 1903 magnum opus, *Sex and Character*. Accepting the antisemitic critique of Jews as valid, both sought not only to distance

38. Ibid., p. 22.

39. Lewin, "Self-Hatred among Jews," pp. 186–87. For the attitudes of German Jews to their east European fellow Jews, see Steven E. Aschheim, *Brothers and Strangers: The East European Jew in German and German Jewish Consciousness, 1800–1923* (Madison: University of Wisconsin Press, 1982).

themselves from their Jewish origins but also to eradicate the feminized Jew within themselves.

As a young man of thirty in 1897, Walther Rathenau published his reflections on the Jewish question anonymously in the journal *Die Zukunft* (The future) in an essay entitled "Hear, O Israel." An assimilated Jew, Rathenau was acutely self-conscious about the persistent otherness of Jews in German society. Highly critical of Jewish behavior, he called upon Jews to remake themselves. Like many antisemites, he commented upon the physical awkwardness of Jews, which could be seen as a type of feminization. "Look in the mirror!" exclaimed Rathenau. "If you recognize your poorly constructed frame—the high shoulders, the clumsy feet, the soft roundedness of form—as signs of bodily decadence, you will, for a few generations, work for your external rebirth."[40]

Born in 1880, Otto Weininger studied at the University of Vienna at a time when it was rife with antisemitism. A brilliant and precocious student, he converted to Protestantism upon receiving his doctorate at the age of twenty-two. Weininger's *Sex and Character* combined misogyny and antisemitism in a powerfully charged analysis.[41] For Weininger, women

40. Walther Rathenau, "Höre, Israel!" as cited in Robert A. Pois, "Walther Rathenau's Jewish Quandary," *Leo Baeck Institute Yearbook* 13 (1968): 121. On Rathenau, see James Joll, *Intellectuals in Politics: Three Biographical Essays* (London: Weidenfeld & Nicholson, 1960), pp. 59–129. On Rathenau's conflicted sense of Jewishness, see Solomon Liptzin, *Germany's Stepchildren* (1944; reprint, Cleveland and New York: Meridian Books, 1961), pp. 139–51.

41. Otto Weininger, *Sex and Character* (London: William Heinemann; New York: G. Putnam's Sons, 1906; reprint of the authorized translation of 6th German ed., New York: AMS Press, 1975). For a recent analysis

and men were polar opposites. Women had no selves; defined by their sexuality, they existed only in relation to men. Jews also represented a negative element in Western culture. In Weininger's terms Jews were among those "nations and races whose men . . . are found to approach so slightly and so rarely to the ideal of manhood." Indeed, he found Judaism to be "saturated with femininity, with precisely those qualities the essence of which [are] . . . in the strongest opposition to the male nature." Like women, Jews had no personalities of their own, no moral sensibility, no souls, no capacity for genius; their mode of argument was circular and their aesthetic sense defective.[42]

> The congruity between Jews and women further reveals itself in the extreme adaptability of the Jews, in their great talent for journalism, the "mobility" of their minds, their lack of deeply-rooted and original ideas, in fact the mode in which, like women, because they are nothing in themselves, they can become everything. The Jew . . . is in constant close relation with the lower life, and has no share in the higher metaphysical life.[43]

For Weininger Jewishness, femininity, and masculinity were Platonic ideas, cultural types that could be found outside the

---

of Weininger's work, see Jacques Le Rider, *Le cas Otto Weininger: Racines de l'antiféminisme et de l'antisémitisme* (Paris: Presses Universitaires de France, 1982). Weininger was one of six case studies in Lessing's work on self-hatred. Indeed, Weininger used the term in his own writing. See Lessing, *Der jüdischer Selbsthass*, pp. 80–100, and Le Rider, *Le cas Otto Weininger*, p. 202. On Weininger, also see Liptzin, *Germany's Stepchildren*, pp. 184–89, and Mosse, *Crisis of German Ideology*, p. 215.

42. Weininger, *Sex and Character*, pp. 302, 306, 307–9, 313, 316. See also Gilman, *Jewish Self-Hatred*, p. 247.

43. Weininger, *Sex and Character*, p. 320.

Jew, the woman, or the man. Thus, he could conclude, "Judaism is the spirit of modern life. . . . Our age is not only the most Jewish, but the most feminine."[44] Disgusted with the ineradicable female and Jewish traits that he found within himself, Weininger acted upon the logic of his philosophy that condemned these characteristics and committed suicide shortly after completing his book. Subsequently *Sex and Character* was translated into several languages, went through thirty German editions, and influenced the emerging field of psychology.

Although Weininger and Rathenau do not typify the responses of Jewish men to the antisemites' cultural denial of their masculinity, their radical discourse points to issues that lay beneath the surface of the Western Jewish community's sexual politics. Since the gendered division of assimilation served to reinforce the linkage of Jewishness and feminine characteristics, Jewish men doubtless felt a need to distinguish themselves from women and to eliminate any hint of the feminine in their self-presentation.

As I have already pointed out, the acculturation and integration of Jews in Western societies transformed the prescribed roles of both men and women, but their impact upon men was far greater than upon women. The Jewish expression and identity of men were reduced in scope. Once they absented themselves from regular attendance at the synagogue and substituted secular education for Torah study, they undermined the pillars of traditional Jewish masculinity. Although they continued to run the institutions of the Jewish community, the measure of their success was taken in the larger society. Indeed, their position in the Jewish community often depended upon their achievements outside the community.

44. Ibid., p. 329.

Jewish women in the West, on the other hand, experienced not the diminution of their Jewish roles but their expansion. To be sure, their level of ritual observance, like Jewish men's, fell, though apparently at a slower rate. But they experienced their Judaism, however much its content had changed, as they always had—embedded in a domestic context. Because bourgeois society celebrated women's domestic spirituality, the Jewish expression of female Jews was reinforced in the West, at a time when male Jews experienced considerable tension between their daily lives in a Christian-dominated society and their Jewishness. Jewish women acquired a new role that was ostensibly highly valued, the role of transmitters of Jewish culture to their children. They were now held responsible for maintaining the integrity of the Jewish family as the locus of the formation of Jewish identity.[45]

The representations of women that appear in Jewish communal literature reflect Jewish men's profound ambivalence about this transfer of responsibility within Jewish families, the enhancement of women's status as guardians of Jewishness, and the further conflation of Jewishness and femaleness. The analysis that I present here is necessarily suggestive rather than definitive; but it explains much of the paradox of the communal criticism of women in Western Jewish communities, even though females were less assimilated than their male peers. In their communal critique of Jewish mothers, male Jewish leaders did not acknowledge the newness of the prescribed female role; Jewish women had always been the agents of cultural transmission within the community, they argued. Yet in

45. For a discussion of this phenomenon in Imperial Germany, see Kaplan, The Making of the Jewish Middle Class, pp. 64–84.

criticizing mothers for failing to transfer Jewish knowledge to their sons, they were covertly expressing anxiety about the shift of the task of Jewish cultural transmission from the public (male) domain to the private (female) domain. Most importantly, they revealed an unresolved conflict about their own loss of traditional Jewish learning and status. They were not compensated for this loss, as they had expected, by their achievements in the larger society, because their mobility was accompanied by a flourishing social and cultural antisemitism. Indeed, the eruption of antisemitism in the last quarter of the nineteenth century, at a time when most Jews anticipated its elimination as they realized the project of assimilation, shocked Jewish men who had successfully negotiated economic and social barriers to enter into the middle class. The social and psychological vulnerability of Jewish men in late-nineteenth-century Western societies heightened among them the critique of women that was common in bourgeois societies in general. By stressing the strength required to battle for economic success and support their families, Jewish men also found in their identity as men the power that they could not have as Jews in the larger society.

These themes appear with regularity not only in the Jewish press but even in vernacular Jewish prayer books. A popular, rabbinic-authored, French-language prayer book, first published in 1848 and subsequently translated into several languages and reprinted for decades, highlighted the contrast between male strength and female weakness. The husband prayed in his personal petition, "May I never forget that if might and reason are the perquisite of my sex, hers is subject to bodily weakness and to spiritual sensitivity. . . . May her weakness even serve as a stay against my might; for it would be cruel to abuse a weak and delicate being whom love and law have placed under my protection."[46] Although the male Jew no longer exceeded his wife in a substantial way in Jewish learning, he could take pride in surpassing her in physical strength, reason, and legal status.

The tensions surrounding gender and Jewish identity that were most visible in Western middle-class life at the end of the last century surfaced again in the United States in the generation that was born in the decades following the First World War. By then the immigrant task of Americanization was largely accomplished. Second- and third-generation American Jews of east European origin experienced a social and economic mobility outstripping that of any other immigrant group that arrived on American shores in the same era of mass migration.[47] By the 1920s American Jewish elites no longer placed the promotion of Americanization at the top of their communal agenda. Mass migration had ended, and immigrant Jews and especially their children were accommodating with all due speed to the exigencies of American life. Instead, Jewish leaders identified as a central issue of concern the transmission of Judaism and a Jewish identity to American-born youth. This new goal would be met

46. Arnaud Aron, *Prières d'un coeur israélite: Receuil de prières et de méditations pour toutes les circonstances de la vie* (Strasbourg: Imprimerie de G. Silbermann, 1848), p. 263.

47. On the socioeconomic mobility of Jewish immigrants to America, see Arcadius Kahan, "Economic Opportunities and Some Pilgrims' Progress: Jewish Immigrants from Eastern Europe in the U.S., 1890–1914," in *Essays in Jewish Social and Economic History*, ed. Roger Weiss (Chicago: University of Chicago Press, 1986), pp. 101–17, and Thomas Kessner, *The Golden Door: Italian and Jewish Immigrant Mobility in New York City, 1880–1915* (New York: Oxford University Press, 1977).

by strengthening Jewish educational institutions and by promoting among mothers a special responsibility for creating and sustaining a Jewish home. Consequently, in middle-class American families in the middle third of the twentieth century, as in middle-class central and western European families in the last third of the nineteenth century, regular expression of Jewishness was increasingly relegated to the female domain of the home and specifically identified with women.

It should come as no surprise, then, that American Jewish men struggling with the role of gender and Jewishness in the formation of their identities as adult Americans would inscribe their struggle upon the character of women, and particularly upon their mothers. From the 1930s through 1947 their struggle to define themselves as Jewish men coincided with a peak period of antisemitism in America. The emergence of the demeaning negative caricature of the Jewish mother in the years after World War II was an American manifestation of Jewish self-hatred, more moderate than its European predecessor but also forged in response to antisemitism. European exponents of Jewish self-hatred linked Jewishness with feminine characteristics and directed their attack against Jewish men, indeed often against themselves, for harboring ineradicable elements of otherness, both ethnic and gendered. In America, Jewish men displaced their self-hatred; denying it, they directed their critique at Jewish women. The characteristics that they mocked could be presented as female, rather than as Jewish, qualities. Because the object of derision was female and the disseminator of the stereotype was himself a Jew, the ethnic target was masked. As one sociologist demonstrated in her study of Jewish-authored jokebooks, both the narrators and the male audience of the disparaging Jewish-mother jokes that circulated in the years after the Second World War could perceive the jokes as "instances of sympathetic in-group humor" because they did not stress the Jewishness of the female target of the humor.[48]

Yet the anxiety that found expression in jokes about, and in negative literary portraits of, Jewish women revolved precisely around the perceived connection of gender and Jewishness in American Jewish life. Cultural anthropologist Riv-Ellen Prell posits that the stereotypes of Jewish women "symbolize, through one gender's perspective, the association of sexuality, acculturation, family, and consumption, the key themes of American Judaism in the post-war period."[49] Living in a period of prosperity and assimilation, American Jewish men confronted competing pressures: to sally forth from their homes and achieve success and acceptance in the larger society and yet to maintain their ties to their families and religio-ethnic origins. Women came to symbolize the conflicts inherent in the definition of American Jewish success, for women were represented as the ones who sought both material affluence and Jewish continuity in the home. Mothers and wives de-

48. Gladys Rothbell, "The Jewish Mother: Social Construction of a Popular Image," in *The Jewish Family: Myths and Reality*, ed. Steven M. Cohen and Paula E. Hyman (New York: Holmes & Meier, 1986), pp. 120, 123–24, 126. The quotation is from p. 126.

49. Riv-Ellen Prell, "Rage and Representation: Jewish Gender Stereotypes in American Culture," in *Uncertain Terms: Negotiating Gender in American Culture*, ed. Faye Ginsburg and Anna Lowenhaupt Tsing (Boston: Beacon Press, 1990), p. 262. For an analysis of the JAP (Jewish American princess) stereotype, which lies beyond the scope of this book since it became a full-blown representation of Jewish women only in the 1970s, see Riv-Ellen Prell, "Why Jewish Princesses Don't Sweat: Desire and Consumption in Postwar American Jewish Culture," in *People of the Body: Jews and Judaism from an Embodied Perspective*, ed. Howard Eilberg-Schwartz (Albany: State University of New York Press, 1992), pp. 329–59.

manded that their male kin prevail in the struggle for affluence in society at large and yet they set strict limits to male assimilation—particularly by urging them to resist Gentile women. As agents of acculturation, Jewish mothers articulated the goals of Americanization in terms of the acquisition of secular education and professional status. As newly authorized transmitters of Jewish culture, they symbolically maintained the boundaries, preventing their sons from fully entering into the American mainstream.

The previously celebrated emotional strength and fierce determination of the Jewish mother of eastern European origins, as seen now by her third-generation sons, pointed to an inversion of conventional notions of male-female relations. According to middle-class Western norms, a docile wife deferred to her dominant husband. Yet the controlling and smothering Jewish mother depicted by Jewish novelists and comedians undermined the masculinity of her sons along with that of her husband. Philip Roth's self-pitying Alexander Portnoy fantasizes himself as a child saying to his father, "Deck her, Jake. Surely that's what a *goy* would do, would he not? . . . Poppa, why do we have to have such guilty deference to women—you and me—when we don't! We mustn't! Who should run the show, Poppa, is us!"[50] The very strength of the Jewish mother was a sign of the incomplete Americanization of her family. The disparagement of Jewish mothers paralleled an attack on American mothers that began during World War II and continued into the cold war; both Jewish and Gentile mothers were called to task for smothering their sons emotionally and failing to raise them as proper

50. Philip Roth, *Portnoy's Complaint* (1969; reprint, New York: Bantam House, 1970), pp. 97–98.

men.[51] The Jewish critique, however, derived from specific concerns about Jewish assimilation and identity. It linked the Jewish mother to two elements of Jewish identity that constrained masculine behavior and especially the Jewish man's free choice of sexual partner: the psychosocial, ethnic aspects of identity, as manifested in the family, and the religiocultural dimensions of Jewishness, as expressed in the female sphere of the home.

The discourse of gender and identity in both the European and the American Jewish communities, as I have so far identified it, was largely shaped by men and represented the tensions they experienced in negotiating their own identity in different societal contexts. Did Jewish women make no contribution to the sexual politics of Jewish identity in the modern world? This is a hard question to answer with any confidence, for Jewish women, like other women, have left behind fewer sources for an exploration of their consciousness than have men.

The development of Jewish women's organizations and the activities of prominent female leaders in the past century, however, provide indirect evidence that Jewish women saw in the prevailing modern gender division of responsibilities an opportunity to assert their own centrality to Jewish communal life. They embraced the responsibility of cultural transmission and of maintaining the boundaries inherent in the project of assimilation. In other words, the increased iden-

---

51. For the classic statement of "momism," see Philip Wylie, *Generation of Vipers* (New York: Holt, Rinehart & Winston, 1942). On the social implications of the critique of American mothers, see Elaine Tyler May, *Homeward Bound: American Families in the Cold War Era* (New York: Basic Books, 1988).

tification of Jewishness and femaleness that induced anxiety among Jewish men enabled Jewish women to lay claim to new public roles.

Although the roles and representation of Jewish women in the West and in eastern Europe differed considerably, Jewish leaders in the modern world increasingly recognized that women's education could not be left to chance. Whether to retain the loyalty of Jewish girls and/or to prepare them for the hallowed task of educating their children, the Jewish community would have to upgrade the education offered to its female members and thereby diminish the "learning gap" between men and women.

As individuals and as leaders of women's organizations, Jewish women devoted themselves to the Jewish education of their own sex as a means of empowerment, even as they acknowledged that women had a special role to play as the first and most important instructors of their children. In establishing the first middle school for Jewish girls in Warsaw, Puah Rakowski was among the earliest of Jewish women educators to create an educational institution designed expressly for female students. Although she considered the lack of Jewish education accorded women in traditional Jewish society a disaster for the Jewish people because of the mother's role in transmitting a cultural identity to her children, she also focused on the education of Jewish girls for their own sake. As she wrote in her memoirs, she felt "an inner obligation to struggle for the liberation of the woman, in particular the Jewish woman. . . . In woman's economic independence [which would be secured through education] I saw the central factor that would lead to her personal and social liberation." Her commitment to women's education was linked to her dedication to Jewish survival, for she became involved in the Zionist cause upon her arrival in Warsaw in 1891.[52] Her own story also demonstrates that education could provide a woman with personal empowerment as well as with the ability to support herself and her family; she clearly had those goals for her students as well.

Almost fifty years later in New York City in 1933, Trude Weiss-Rosmarin, a new immigrant from Germany with a doctorate in Semitics, archeology, and philosophy, founded the School of the Jewish Woman as an institution of adult education. Her rationale was similar to Rakowski's, though expressed initially in less radical terms.[53] In a pamphlet written in the early years of the school and entitled *Jewish Women and Jewish Culture*, Weiss-Rosmarin promoted women's education on the well-trodden ground that "in our day, the duty of education has been entirely transferred to the mother. Hers is the responsibility both for the physical and for the mental and Jewish upbringing of the young generation."[54] But the Jewish mother could not meet her responsibilities unless she were herself educated in Jewish culture. Weiss-Rosmarin went further, however, arguing that Jewish education was important not only for the sake of the Jewish

52. Rakowski, *Zikhroynes*, pp. 19, 62–64, 67–69. The quotation is from p. 64. On the impact of Rakowski's school, see Rosenthal-Shnaiderman, *Oyf vegn un umvegn*, 1:290–91.

53. Deborah Dash Moore, "Trude Weiss-Rosmarin and *The Jewish Spectator*," *Jewish Spectator*, Spring 1993, pp. 8–15. The school was operated initially under the auspices of Hadassah.

54. Trude Weiss-Rosmarin, *Jewish Women and Jewish Culture* (New York: School of the Jewish Woman, n.d.), p. 2. I wish to thank Deborah Dash Moore for graciously providing me with a copy of the document. Moore considers 1936 a plausible publication date.

woman's children "but also for her own self," to provide her with a "fixed center."[55] To accomplish that goal the School of the Jewish Woman offered a curriculum that presumed that Jewish women should, and could, acquire the Jewish knowledge available to Jewish men in modern institutions of higher learning: Hebrew language, Jewish history, Bible, Talmud, customs and ceremonies, liturgy, and philosophy. It also equipped students for professional work in Jewish education, offering a Sunday School teacher's diploma and credits that public-school teachers could use toward a salary increment.[56] Although the primary justification for the education of women was derived from a division of gender roles rooted in the woman's maternal responsibilities, female education also served other needs and expanded women's roles. Similarly, the Sholom Aleichem Women's Clubs articulated the need for the education of Jewish mothers so that they could promote a love of Yiddish and foster a progressive national consciousness in their children.

The multiple implications for Jewish communal life of educating women became most apparent in the activity of Jewish women's organizations. In the United States, the National Council of Jewish Women, Hadassah, and national organizations of sisterhoods and, in Great Britain, the Union of Jewish Women addressed the issue of providing Jewish education for their own members, while in Germany Bertha Pappenheim, founder and leader of the Jüdischer Frauenbund, regularly called for enhanced Jewish education for women.[57]

55. Ibid., pp. 4–5. The quotations are from p. 5.

56. Ibid., pp. 6–8.

57. See Rogow, *Gone to Another Meeting*, pp. 59–72; Joan Dash, *Summoned to Jerusalem: The Life of Henrietta Szold* (New York: Harper & Row, 1979); Kuz-

All of these organizations, with the exception of Orthodox sisterhoods, moved from the call for significant education for women to the assertion of women's claim to equal rights within communal institutions and/or the synagogue. The Jüdischer Frauenbund, for example, campaigned vigorously for female suffrage within the Gemeinde, the formal communal organization of German Jewry in every locale. The National Council of Jewish Women asserted its right to autonomy in managing substantial funds for social welfare work. The Union of Jewish Women in 1904 gained the support of the London Jewish Chronicle for a "more responsible position" for Jewish women "in communal work and counsels" on the basis of its effective philanthropic and educational activity. As already noted, Reform sisterhood leaders spoke openly in the 1930s of full equality for women within the synagogue, and the Women's League for Conservative Judaism was instrumental in the creation of a Women's Institute of Jewish Studies.[58] In all of these cases the rhetoric of domestic feminism broke down the boundaries between the home, in which the Jewish woman's primary responsibilities were presumed to lie, and the public sphere of formal education, communal politics, and social welfare. Through their volunteer organizations Jewish women carried the banner of "cultural transmission" from the home into the streets and embellished its message to

---

mack, Woman's Cause, pp. 49–50; and Kaplan, The Jewish Feminist Movement in Germany, pp. 50, 115.

58. Kaplan, The Jewish Feminist Movement in Germany, pp. 151–65; Baum, Hyman, and Michel, The Jewish Woman in America, pp. 175–78. On the council's substantial social welfare activity, see Rogow, Gone to Another Meeting, pp. 130–66; Kuzmack, Woman's Cause, p. 50; Nadell, "Religious Emancipation," esp. p. 11.

include concern for Jewish survival broadly conceived along with teaching Jewish morality and customs to one's own children.

We have seen that Jewish men and women experienced the process of assimilation in different social contexts wherever they lived and followed different gendered prescriptions of appropriate behavior. As they assumed the mantle of cultural transmitters, did women articulate a vision of Judaism and Jewishness that differed in any appreciable way from the contemporary versions of Judaism promulgated by rabbis and male lay leaders? Such a disparity, it can be assumed, would have had two consequences. It would have exacerbated the tensions experienced by men seeking to define an appropriate Jewish identity for themselves; and it would have fed the resentment of women, whose power within Jewish communal institutions was minimal, despite their duly acknowledged responsibility for ensuring the survival of Jews and Judaism.

Several feminist scholars have suggested that Jewish women articulated a particularly female form of spirituality that was personal in tone and not based in traditional prayer or study. According to their analysis, in the modern period some Jewish women have framed their social reform or Zionist activities in terms of a religious mission, in which public expression of moral behavior testified to spiritual commitment. Others, who saw themselves as religious leaders, envisioned an awareness of and communion with God as the focus of their spiritual lives and deemed women's spirituality to be different from men's.[59] For example, Martha Neumark, the daughter of

59. Rogow, *Gone to Another Meeting*, pp. 158–59; Ellen Umansky, "Spiritual Expressions: Jewish Women's Religious Lives in the Twentieth-Century United States," in *Jewish Women in Historical Perspective*, ed. Judith Baskin

a faculty member, attended Hebrew Union College and, after completing the rabbinic curriculum, petitioned in 1923 to be ordained a rabbi, a request ultimately denied. She offered as one rationale for the ordination of women that the "spiritual struggles" of a woman would be closer and of greater interest to women, who composed the majority of worshipers in the Reform synagogue.[60] Such a claim, however, provides little evidence of any substantive difference between Jewish men's and women's struggles.

In her work on Lily Montagu, a lay minister in England's movement of Liberal Judaism, and on Tehilla Lichtenstein, a cofounder of Jewish Science, Ellen Umansky has suggested that these two women leaders based their teaching on personal intuition and everyday experience. She sees a possible connection between their religious stance and traditional Jewish women's religiosity, which may have been associated with inner piety.[61] Despite Umansky's suggestion, however, I have not yet seen in the writings of modern women who preceded contemporary Jewish feminism any themes or style that clearly distinguish their historical and theological reflec-

---

(Detroit: Wayne State University Press, 1991), pp. 266–74, 278–83; and Umansky, *Lily Montagu and the Advancement of Liberal Judaism.*

60. Martha Neumark, "The Woman Rabbi," *Jewish Tribune,* 17 April 1925, p. 5, as quoted in Ann D. Braude, "Jewish Women in the Twentieth Century: Building a Life in America," in *Women and Religion in America,* vol. 3, 1900–1968, ed. Rosemary Radford Ruether and Rosemary Skinner Keller (San Francisco: Harper & Row, 1986), p. 164.

61. Ellen Umansky, "Piety, Persuasion and Friendship: Jewish Female Leadership in Modern Times," in *Embodied Love: Sensuality and Relationship as Feminist Values,* ed. Paula M. Cooey, Sharon A. Farmer, and Mary Ellen Ross (New York: Harper & Row, 1987), pp. 189–206.

tions from those prevalent in the denominations with which they were affiliated. Their emphasis on the ethical and on emotional spirituality within Judaism seems to reflect the fact that most of the Jewish women writers on Judaism have been affiliated with the Reform or Liberal movements in Judaism.

Historians of the east European immigrant generations in America have addressed the secular, rather than the religious, dimensions of women's changing roles. They have posited the emergence of a "New Jewish Womanhood" that built upon the intersection of secular Jewish culture with American conditions of female labor and politics.[62] Secularization, the employment of young women for wages, and the union movement, in the words of historian Susan Glenn, "encouraged young women to feel optimistic about making relationships based on a partnership between the sexes" and "strengthened and legitimated the female presence in the affairs of the community."[63] The growing participation of Jewish women in communal affairs as well as in American civic life in subsequent generations built upon the sense of civic responsibility, opportunity, and legitimacy of female political activism engendered in the immigrant communities.

As contemporary Jewish feminism, which arose some two decades ago, continues to develop and affect American Jewry, it will be important to see whether and how feminist spirituality influences the ways in which Jewish women express their Judaism and whether and how feminist activism influences the roles Jewish women play in communal and Ameri-

62. For the most recent and most comprehensive exploration of this issue, see Glenn, *Daughters of the Shtetl*, pp. 207–42.

63. Ibid., p. 210.

can civic life.[64] Scholars and communal leaders alike will also have to be alert to the responses of Jewish communal institutions to the new roles and self-definitions of women as American Jews seek to shape an identity for the twenty-first century. To what extent will the growing visibility of women in the public realm of Jewish communal life increase the identification of women with Judaism and thereby exacerbate the sexual politics of contemporary Jewish identity? In the absence of significant antisemitism, will the sexual politics of Jewish identity necessarily be muted? To what extent will Jewish women choose to invest their energy primarily in those institutions of the larger society that have accepted gender equality as a fundamental aspect of modern life?

For modern Jews, living in societies that promised (and often delivered) the prizes of civic equality and access to the cultural wealth of Western civilization, both the process and the project of assimilation have been gendered. Jewish men and women have confronted the challenges of Western society on different turfs. As they constructed Jewish identities appropriate to their circumstances, their behavior also differed because they experienced the process of assimilation differently. Because the dominant cultural model for European and American Jews has been middle class, Jewish thinkers and communal leaders have promoted gender roles reflective of the bourgeois ideal: men in the public sphere, women

64. On contemporary Jewish feminist spirituality, see Judith Plaskow, Standing Again at Sinai (San Francisco: Harper & Row, 1990), and Susannah Heschel, ed., On Being a Jewish Feminist (New York: Schocken Books, 1983). For an analysis of the impact of feminism on American Jewish life, see Sylvia Barack Fishman, A Breath of Life: Feminism in the American Jewish Community (New York: Free Press, 1993).

in the domestic sphere; men responsible for the secular business of running society, women responsible for the inculcation of moral and religious values. The project of assimilation, which was essentially a Western phenomenon intimately linked to bourgeois culture, also differentiated between male and female roles. Presuming that entry into the larger society would be accompanied by the survival of Jews and Judaism, it placed the burden of setting limits to assimilation upon women. In doing so, it expanded women's opportunities for acquiring Jewish education, for exploring the meaning of their Jewishness, and for carrying their "domestic" responsibilities into the public domain of social welfare. But it also inadvertently promoted among Jewish men the identification of Judaism with women. Faced with the need to establish their own identities in societies in which they were both fully acculturated and yet perceived as partially Other because they were Jews, Jewish men were eager to distinguish themselves from the women of their community, whom they saw as the guardians of Jewishness. The negative representations of women that they produced reflected their own ambivalence about assimilation and its limits. Exploring gender differences in behavior and representation and laying bare the sexual politics of Jewish identity permit us, therefore, to understand more clearly the challenges of Jewish self-definition in the modern world.

# Bibliography

## PRIMARY SOURCES

### Books and Articles

Aguilar, Grace. *The Women of Israel*. 2 vols. in 1. New York: D. Appleton & Co., 1851.

Aleichem, Sholom. *Selected Stories of Sholom Aleichem*. New York: Random House, Modern Library, 1956.

Antin, Mary. *The Promised Land*. 1912. Reprint, Boston: Houghton-Mifflin, 1969.

Aron, Arnaud. *Prières d'un coeur israélite: Receuil de prières et de méditations pour toutes les circonstances de la vie*. Strasbourg: Imprimerie de G. Silbermann, 1848.

Asch, Scholem. *The Mother*. Trans. Nathan Ausubel. New York: Liveright, 1930.

Bas Yonah [Sheyndl Dvorin]. *Em labanim: (Zikhronotai)* (A mother of children: [My memories]). Pinsk: Druk Dolinko, 1935.

Berg, Rebecca Himber. "Childhood in Lithuania." In *Memoirs of My People*, ed. Leo Schwarz. New York: Schocken, 1963.

Bergner, Hinda [Rosenblatt]. *In di lange vinternekht: Mishpokhe zikhroynes fun a shtetl in Galizie, 1870–1900* (In the long winter nights: Family memories from a shtetl in Galicia, 1870–1900). Montreal: privately published, 1946.

Berlin-Papish, Tova. *Ẓelilim shelo nishkḥu: Mimohilev ʿad Yerushalayim* (Sounds that were not forgotten: From Mohilev to Jerusalem). Tel Aviv: Reshafim, 1988.

Berman, Zehava. *Bedarki sheli* (In my own way). Jerusalem: Elyashar, 1982.

Berr, Berr Isaac. "Lettre d'un citoyen, membre de la ci-devant Communauté des Juifs de Lorraine, à ses confrères, à l'occasion du droit du Citoyen actif, rendu aux Juifs par le décret du 28 septembre 1791." Nancy, 1791. Reprinted in *La Révolution française et l'émancipation des Juifs*, vol. 8 (Paris: Editions d'Histoire Sociale, 1968).

Blaustein, David. *Memoirs of David Blaustein: Educator and Communal Worker*. Arranged by Miriam Blaustein. New York: McBride, Nast & Co., 1913.

Cahan, Abraham. *The Rise of David Levinsky*. New York: Harper & Brothers, 1917.

——— . *Yekl: A Tale of the New York Ghetto*. New York: D. Appleton & Co., 1896.

Chagall, Bella. *Burning Lights*. 1946. Reprint, New York: Schocken Press, 1962.

Cohen, Rose. *Out of the Shadow*. New York: George H. Doran Co., 1918.

Dinur, Bilhah. *Lenechdotai: Zikhronot mishpaḥah vesipurei ḥavayot* (For my granddaughters: Family memories and stories of experiences). Arranged and edited by Ben Zion Dinur. Jerusalem: privately printed, 1972.

Edelman, Fanny. *Der shpigel fun leben* (The mirror of my life). New York: Shulsinger Brothers Printers, 1948.

Edelstein, Zelda. *Bedarkhei avot* (In the ways of the fathers). Jerusalem: privately printed, 1970.

Fogelman, Bella. *Mibeit aba ʿad halom* (From my father's house to here). Kiryat Motzkin: privately printed, 1974.

*Di froy in der heym un in shop: Aroysgebn fun fareyniktn kaunsil un arbeter klas hoyz-froyen*. 4 pp. New York, [1926?].

*Froyen-shul "Yehudiyah" in Vilna*. Vilna: B. Kletzkin, 1913.

Gold, Michael. *Jews without Money*. New York: Horace Liveright, 1930. Reprint, New York: Avon Books, 1965.

Guber, Rivka. *Morasha lehanḥil* (A legacy to pass on). Jerusalem: Kiryat Sefer, 1981.

Hapgood, Hutchins. *The Spirit of the Ghetto*. 1902. Reprint, New York: Schocken Books, 1966.

Heinman, Malka. *Zikhronot shel Malka* (Memoirs of Malka). Jerusalem: privately printed, 1983.

Herzl, Theodor. *Old-New Land ("Altneuland")*. Trans. Lotta Levenson.

1941. Reprint, New York: Markus Wiener Publishing and Herzl Press, 1987. First published, in German, in 1902.

Di idishe froy. Aroysgegebn fun di Sholom Aleichem Froyen Klubn, vol. 1, no. 1, Nov. 1925.

Jastrow, Marie. A Time to Remember: Growing up in New York before the Great War. New York: Norton, 1979.

Kalish, Ita. Etmolai (My yesterdays). Tel Aviv: Hakibutz Hameuchad Publishing House, 1970.

Kallen, Horace. Culture and Democracy in the United States. New York: Boni & Liveright, 1924.

Kaplan-Merminski, Rokhl. Froyen-problem. Warsaw, 1927.

Kazin, Alfred. A Walker in the City. New York: Harcourt, Brace, 1951.

Kirshenbaum, Haya. Zikhronot me ʿir huladti, Meliẓ (Memories from the city of my birth, Melitz). N.p., n.d. Published by family after the author's death in 1976.

Kohut, Rebekah [Bettelheim]. "Jewish Women's Organizations in the United States." American Jewish Yearbook 5692, vol. 33. Philadelphia: Jewish Publication Society, 1931.

————. More Yesterdays. New York: Bloch Publishing Co., 1950.

————. My Portion (An Autobiography). New York: Albert & Charles Boni, 1927.

Korngold, Sheyna. Zikhroynes (Memoirs). Tel Aviv: Farlag Idpress, 1970.

Kositza, Rokhl. Zikhroynes fun a bialystoker froy (Memoirs of a woman from Białystok). Los Angeles: Schwartz Printing Co., 1964.

Kramer, Sydelle, and Jenny Masur, eds. Jewish Grandmothers. Boston: Beacon Press, 1976.

Lishensky, Shoshana. Miẓror zikhronotai (From the bouquet of my memories). Jerusalem: Dfus Merkaz, 1942.

Malitz, Chaim. Di heym un di froy. New York: n.p., 1918.

Manning, Caroline. The Immigrant Woman and Her Job. Washington: U.S. Government Printing Office, 1930.

Marcus, Jacob Rader, ed. The American Jewish Woman: A Documentary History. New York and Cincinnati: Ktav Publishing House and American Jewish Archives, 1981.

Melamed, Deborah. The Three Pillars: Thought, Worship and Practice for the

# Bibliography

*Jewish Woman*. New York: Women's League of the United Synagogue of America, 1927.

Melamed, Frances Senior. *Janova*. Cincinnati: Janova Press, 1976.

Metzker, I., ed. *A Bintel Brief*. Garden City, N.Y.: Doubleday, 1971.

Meyer, Annie Nathan. *It's Been Fun*. New York: Henry Schuman, 1951.

Montagu, Lily. *Lily Montagu: Sermons, Letters, Addresses and Prayers*. Ed. Ellen M. Umansky. Lewiston, N.Y.: Edwin Mellen, 1985.

Morgenstern, Joseph. *I Have Considered My Days*. New York: Yiddish Kultur Farband, 1964.

Nathan, Maud. *Once upon a Time and Today*. New York and London: G. P. Putnam's Sons, 1933.

Neuda, Fanny. *Stunden der Andacht*. 1857. Prague: W. Pascheles, 1868.

Nordau, Max. *Degeneration*. Trans. from 2d ed. of German work. New York: D. Appleton, 1895.

———. *Ecrits sionistes*. Ed. Baruch Hagani. Paris: Librairie Lipschutz, 1936.

———. *Zionistische Schriften*. Cologne and Leipzig: Jüdischer Verlag, 1909.

Odets, Clifford. *Awake and Sing!* New York: Random House, 1935.

Pappenheim, Bertha, and Sara Rabinowitsch. *Zur Lage der jüdischen Bevölkerung in Galizien: Reise-Eindrücke und Vorschläge zur Besserung der Verhältnisse*. Frankfurt am Main: Neuer Frankfurter Verlag, 1904.

Pesotta, Rose. *Days of Our Lives*. New York: Excelsior, 1958.

Rakowski, Puah. "Di froyen oyf di minsker asefo" (Women at the Minsk meeting). *Di yudishe froyenvelt* 13 (24 Sept. 1902): 1–3.

——— [Rakowska]. *Di moderne froyen-bavegung*. Warsaw, 1928.

——— [Rakowska]. *Di yiddishe froy*. Warsaw: Bnos Tsiyon, 1918.

———. *Zikhroynes fun a yiddisher revolutsionerin* (Memoirs of a Jewish revolutionary woman). Buenos Aires: Tsentral-Farband fun Poylishe Yidn in Argentina, 1954.

Rosenthal-Shnaiderman, Esther. *Oyf vegn un umvegn: Zikhroynes, geshe ᶜeneshn, perzenlekhkeytn* (Of roads and detours: Memories, events, personalities). 3 vols. Tel Aviv: Farlag "Hamenora," 1974–82.

Roth, Philip. *Portnoy's Complaint*. 1969. Reprint, New York: Bantam House, 1970.

# Bibliography

Rubinraut, H. *Yiddishe froy, dervakh! Vi azoy zikh tsu farhitn fun umgevun-shener shvangershaft* (Jewish woman, awake! How to avoid unwanted pregnancy). Warsaw: Toz, [1934?].

Ruether, Rosemary Radford, and Rosemary Skinner Keller, eds. *Women and Religion in America*, vol. 3, 1900–1968. San Francisco: Harper & Row, 1986.

Ruskay, Esther. *Hearth and Home Essays*. Philadelphia: Jewish Publication Society of America, 1902.

Schwarz, Leo, ed. *Memoirs of My People*. New York: Schocken Press, 1963.

Shazar, Rachel Katznelson. *The Plough Woman: Memoirs of the Pioneer Women of Palestine*. Trans. Maurice Samuel. 1932. Reprint, New York: Herzl Press, 1975.

Simon, Kate. *Bronx Primitive: Portraits in a Childhood*. New York: Harper & Row, 1982.

Sokolow, Nahum. *Idishe froy*. London: English Zionist Federation, 1917.

Sperber, Miriam. *Miberdichev ʿad Yerushalayim: Zikhronot leveit Ruzhin* (From Berdichev to Jerusalem: Recollections of the House of Ruzin). Jerusalem: privately printed, 1981.

Tashrak [Israel Joseph Zevin]. *Etikete*. New York: Hebrew Publishing Co., 1912.

Thiéry, [Adolphe]. *Dissertation sur cette question: Est-il des moyens de rendre les Juifs plus heureux et plus utiles en France?* Paris, 1788. Reprinted in facsimile in *La Révolution française et l'émancipation des Juifs*, vol. 2. (Paris: Editions d'Histoire Sociale, 1968).

Umansky, Ellen M., and Dianne Ashton, eds. *Four Centuries of Jewish Women's Spirituality—A Sourcebook*. Boston: Beacon Press, 1992.

Van Kleeck, Mary. *Artificial Flower Makers*. New York: Survey Associates, 1913.

——— . *Working Girls in Evening Schools: A Statistical Study*. New York: Survey Associates, 1914.

Weininger, Otto. *Sex and Character*. London: William Heinemann; New York: G. Putnam's Sons, 1906. Reprint of the authorized translation of the 6th German ed., New York: AMS Press, 1975.

Weiss-Rosmarin, Trude. *Jewish Women and Jewish Culture*. New York: School of the Jewish Woman, n.d.

# Bibliography

Wengeroff, Pauline. *Memoiren einer Grossmutter: Bilder aus der Kulturgeschichte der Juden Russlands im 19. Jahrhundert.* Berlin: Verlag von M. Poppelauer, 1913.

Wylie, Philip. *Generation of Vipers.* New York: Holt, Rinehart & Winston, 1942.

Yellin, Ita. *Leẓeʾeẓaʾai* (For my descendants). Jerusalem: Hamaʿarav Printing Press, 1928.

Yezierska, Anzia. *Bread Givers.* Garden City, N.Y.: Doubleday, Doran, 1925. Reprint, New York: Persea Books, 1975.

———. *Hungry Hearts.* Boston and New York: Houghton-Mifflin, 1920.

———. *The Open Cage: An Anzia Yezierska Collection.* Selected and with an introduction by Alice Kessler-Harris. New York: Persea Books, 1979.

———. *Red Ribbon on a White Horse.* New York: Charles Scribner's Sons, 1950.

———. *Salome of the Tenements.* New York: Boni & Liveright, 1923.

*Di yudishe froy un der Tsionizm.* Warsaw: Druckerei "Hazefira," 1918.

## YIVO Archive, New York City

Poland: 2.12, Warsaw, 1926, material on Yehudiyah; 3.19, Warsaw, 1926; 5.11, Baranowicze, 1931; 6.27, Pruzany.

Vilna: no. 2, Baranowicze, undated material on women; no. 42, Warsaw, material on family purity, 1920–37; no. 45, Warsaw, circular letter from Yudishen Froyen-Ferayn, 1928.

Poland-Vilna: no. 45, Warsaw, circular letter from Yudishen Froyen-Ferayn, 18 Dec. 1928, signed by Puah Rakowska.

*Di yudishe froy.* N.p.: Agudas Harabonim b'Polin, 1929.

## Newspapers

*Aḥiasaf* (Warsaw)
*American Hebrew*
*American Jewess*
*Archives israélites*
*Ha-Asif* (Warsaw)
*Ben-Ammi* (Saint Petersburg)
*Ha-Boker Or* (Saint Petersburg)

# Bibliography

Ha-Eshkol (Cracow)

Der Fraynd (Saint Petersburg)

Di Froy (Warsaw, Vilna, Lodz, Lemberg)

Froyen-shtim (Warsaw?)

Froyen-velt (New York, 1913)

Froyen-velt (Warsaw?)

Froyen zhurnal (New York)

Haynt (Warsaw)

Ilustrirte vokh (Warsaw)

Jewish Chronicle (London)

Ha-Karmel (Vilna)

Ha-Kerem (Warsaw)

Kneset ha-Gedolah (Warsaw)

Ha-Maggid (Lyck and later Berlin)

Ha-Meliz (Odessa and later Saint Petersburg)

Ha-Mizpeh (Saint Petersburg)

Ha-Mizrah (Cracow)

Der Moment (Warsaw)

Di naye velt (Warsaw)

Ha-Shahar he-Hadash (Cracow)

Ha-Sharon (Cracow)

Shem ve-yafet (Lvov)

Ha-Shiloah (Cracow)

Univers israélite

Yudishe familye (Cracow)

Di yudishe froyenvelt (Cracow)

## SECONDARY SOURCES

### Books

Adler, Ruth. *Women of the Shtetl—Through the Eyes of Y. L. Peretz*. Rutherford, N.J.: Fairleigh Dickinson University Press, 1980.

Aschheim, Steven E. *Brothers and Strangers: The East European Jew in German and German Jewish Consciousness, 1800–1923*. Madison: University of Wisconsin Press, 1982.

# Bibliography

Baskin, Judith R., ed. *Jewish Women in Historical Perspective*. Detroit: Wayne State University Press, 1991.

Baum, Charlotte, Paula Hyman, and Sonya Michel. *The Jewish Woman in America*. New York: Dial Press, 1976.

Beller, Steven. *Vienna and the Jews, 1867–1938: A Cultural History*. Cambridge: Cambridge University Press, 1989.

Ben-Horin, Meir. *Max Nordau, Philosopher of Human Solidarity*. New York: Conference on Jewish Social Studies, 1956.

Berkowitz, Michael. *Zionist Culture and West European Jewry before the First World War*. Cambridge: Cambridge University Press, 1993.

Bernstein, Deborah. *The Struggle for Equality: Urban Women Workers in Pre-state Israeli Society*. New York: Praeger Publications, 1987.

————, ed. *Pioneers and Homemakers: Jewish Women in Pre-state Israel*. Albany: State University of New York Press, 1992.

Berrol, Selma C. *Julia Richman: A Notable Woman*. Philadelphia: Balch Institute Press, 1993.

Biale, David. *Eros and the Jews: From Biblical Israel to Contemporary America*. New York: Basic Books, 1992.

Birnbaum, Pierre. *Les fous de la République: Histoire politique des Juifs d'Etat de Gambetta à Vichy*. Paris: Arthème Fayard, 1992.

Bristow, Edward. *Prostitution and Prejudice: The Jewish Fight against White Slavery, 1870–1939*. New York: Schocken Books, 1983.

Brym, Robert. *The Jewish Intelligentsia and Russian Marxism*. New York: Schocken Books, 1978.

Cohen, Steven M., and Paula E. Hyman, eds. *The Jewish Family: Myths and Reality*. New York: Holmes & Meier, 1986.

Dash, Joan. *Summoned to Jerusalem: The Life of Henrietta Szold*. New York: Harper & Row, 1979.

Dearborn, Mary V. *Pocahontas's Daughters: Gender and Ethnicity in American Culture*. New York: Oxford University Press, 1986.

Douglas, Ann. *The Feminization of American Culture*. New York: Knopf, 1977.

Dushkin, Alexander M. *Jewish Education in New York City*. New York: Bureau of Jewish Education, 1918.

# Bibliography

Eilberg-Schwartz, Howard, ed. *People of the Body: Jews and Judaism from an Embodied Perspective.* Albany: State University of New York Press, 1992.

Elbaum-Dror, Rachel. *Haḥinukh haʿivri bʾereẓ yisraʾel,* vol. 1. (Hebrew education in the land of Israel). Jerusalem: Yad Yitzhak Ben-Zvi, 1986.

Elwell, Sue Levi. "The Founding and Early Programs of the National Council of Jewish Women: Study and Practice as Jewish Women's Religious Expression." Ph.D. diss., Indiana University, 1982.

Endelman, Todd. *The Jews of Georgian England: Tradition and Change in a Liberal Society.* Philadelphia: Jewish Publication Society, 1979.

——— . *Radical Assimilation in English Jewish History, 1656–1945.* Bloomington: Indiana University Press, 1990.

——— , ed. *Jewish Apostasy in the Modern World.* New York: Holmes & Meier, 1987.

Ewen, Elizabeth. *Immigrant Women in the Land of Dollars: Life and Culture on the Lower East Side, 1890–1925.* New York: Monthly Review Press, 1985.

Feldman, David. *Englishmen and Jews: Social Relations and Political Culture, 1840–1914.* New Haven: Yale University Press, 1994.

Fishman, Sylvia Barack. *A Breath of Life: Feminism in the American Jewish Community.* New York: Free Press, 1993.

——— . *Follow My Footprints: Changing Images of Women in American Jewish Fiction.* Hanover, N.H.: University Press of New England, 1992.

Frankel, Jonathan. *Prophecy and Politics: Socialism, Nationalism, and the Russian Jews, 1862–1917.* Cambridge: Cambridge University Press, 1981.

Gay, Peter. *Freud: A Life for Our Time.* New Haven: Yale University Press, 1988.

Gilman, Sander L. *Jewish Self-Hatred: Anti-Semitism and the Hidden Language of the Jews.* Baltimore: Johns Hopkins University Press, 1986.

——— . *The Jew's Body.* New York and London: Routledge, 1991.

Glanz, Rudolf. *The Jewish Woman in America: Two Female Immigrant Generations, 1820–1929,* vol. 1, *The Eastern European Jewish Woman.* N.p.: Ktav Publishing House and National Council of Jewish Women, 1976.

——— . *The Jewish Woman in America: Two Female Immigrant Generations, 1820–1929,* vol. 2, *The German Jewish Woman.* N.p.: Ktav Publishing House and National Council of Jewish Women, 1976.

# Bibliography

Glenn, Susan. *Daughters of the Shtetl: Life and Labor in the Immigrant Generation*. Ithaca: Cornell University Press, 1990.

Goldscheider, Calvin, and Alan Zuckerman. *The Transformation of the Jews*. Chicago: University of Chicago Press, 1984.

Goodman, Cary. *Choosing Sides: Playground and Street Life on the Lower East Side*. New York: Schocken Books, 1979.

Gordon, Milton. *Assimilation in American Life: The Role of Race, Religion and National Origins*. New York: Oxford University Press, 1964.

Goren, Arthur A. *New York Jews and the Quest for Community: The Kehillah Experiment, 1908–1922*. New York: Columbia University Press, 1970.

Hadda, Janet. *Passionate Women, Passive Men: Suicide in Yiddish Literature*. Albany: State University of New York Press, 1988.

Heilbrun, Carolyn G. *Writing a Woman's Life*. New York: Norton, 1988.

Heinze, Andrew. *Adapting to Abundance: Jewish Immigrants, Mass Consumption, and the Search for American Identity*. New York: Columbia University Press, 1990.

Heller, Celia S. *On the Edge of Destruction: Jews of Poland between the Two World Wars*. New York: Columbia University Press, 1977.

Henriksen, Louise Levitas (with the assistance of Jo Ann Boydston). *Anzia Yezierska: A Writer's Life*. New Brunswick: Rutgers University Press, 1986.

Hertz, Deborah. *Jewish High Society in Old Regime Berlin*. New Haven: Yale University Press, 1988.

Hertz, J. S., ed. *Doires Bundistn*. 2 vols. New York: Ferlag Unser Tsait, 1956.

Heschel, Susannah. *On Being a Jewish Feminist*. New York: Schocken Books, 1983.

Higham, John. *Send These to Me: Jews and Other Immigrants in Urban America*. New York: Atheneum, 1975.

Howe, Irving. *World of Our Fathers: The Journey of the East European Jews to America and the Life They Found and Made*. New York: Simon & Schuster, 1976.

Hyman, Paula E. *The Emancipation of the Jews of Alsace: Acculturation and Tradition in the Nineteenth Century*. New Haven: Yale University Press, 1991.

# Bibliography

Joll, James. *Intellectuals in Politics: Three Biographical Essays*. London: Weidenfeld & Nicholson, 1960.

Joselit, Jenna Weissman. *New York's Jewish Jews: The Orthodox Community in the Interwar Years*. Bloomington: Indiana University Press, 1990.

Kaplan, Marion. *The Jewish Feminist Movement in Germany: The Campaigns of the Jüdischer Frauenbund, 1904–1938*. Westport, Conn.: Greenwood Press, 1979.

———. *The Making of the Jewish Middle Class: Women, Family, and Identity in Imperial Germany*. New York: Oxford University Press, 1991.

Katz, Jacob. *Out of the Ghetto*. Cambridge: Harvard University Press, 1973.

Kessner, Thomas. *The Golden Door: Italian and Jewish Immigrant Mobility in New York City, 1880–1915*. New York: Oxford University Press, 1977.

Kleeblatt, Norman, ed. *The Dreyfus Affair: Art, Truth, Justice*. Berkeley: University of California Press, 1987.

Krause, Corinne Azen. *Grandmothers, Mothers, and Daughters: Oral Histories of Three Generations of Ethnic American Women*. Boston: Twayne Publishers, 1991.

Kuzmack, Linda Gordon. *Woman's Cause: The Jewish Women's Movement in England and the United States, 1881–1933*. Columbus: Ohio State University Press, 1990.

Le Rider, Jacques. *Le cas Otto Weininger: Racines de l'antiféminisme et de l'antisémitisme*. Paris: Presses Universitaires de France, 1982.

Lederhendler, Eli. *The Road to Modern Jewish Politics*. New York: Oxford University Press, 1989.

Lessing, Theodor. *Der jüdischer Selbsthass*. 1930. Reprint, Munich: Mattes & Seitz Verlag, 1984.

Levin, Mordekhai. *Erkhei ḥevrah vekalkalah bʾidiologia shel tekufat hahaskalah* (Social and economic values in the ideology of the Haskalah period). Jerusalem: Mosad Bialik, 1975.

Levine, Louis. *The Women's Garment Workers: A History of the International Ladies' Garment Workers' Union*. New York: B. W. Huebsch, 1924.

Lichtenstein, Diane. *Writing Their Nations: The Tradition of Nineteenth-Century American Jewish Women Writers*. Bloomington: Indiana University Press, 1992.

# Bibliography

Liptzin, Solomon. *Germany's Stepchildren.* 1944. Reprint, Cleveland and New York: Meridian Books, 1961.

Loewenstein, Andrea Freud. *Loathsome Jews and Engulfing Women: Metaphors of Projection in the Works of Wyndham Lewis, Charles Williams, and Graham Greene.* New York: New York University Press, 1993.

Marrus, Michael. *The Politics of Assimilation: A Study of the French Jewish Community at the Time of the Dreyfus Affair.* New York: Oxford University Press, 1971.

May, Elaine Tyler. *Homeward Bound: American Families in the Cold War Era.* New York: Basic Books, 1988.

Mendelsohn, Ezra. *The Jews of East Central Europe between the World Wars.* Bloomington: Indiana University Press, 1983.

————. *Zionism in Poland: The Formative Years, 1915–1926.* New Haven: Yale University Press, 1981.

Meyer, Michael A. *The Origins of the Modern Jew.* Detroit: Wayne State University Press, 1967.

Mintz, Alan. *Banished from Their Father's Table: Loss of Faith and Hebrew Autobiography.* Bloomington: Indiana University Press, 1989.

Modder, Montagu Frank. *The Jew in the Literature of England.* Philadelphia: Jewish Publication Society, 1939.

Moore, Deborah Dash. *At Home in America: Second Generation New York Jews.* New York: Columbia University Press, 1981.

Mosse, George. *The Crisis of German Ideology: Intellectual Origins of the Third Reich.* New York: Grosset & Dunlap, 1964.

————. *Nationalism and Sexuality: Respectability and Abnormal Sexuality in Modern Europe.* New York: Howard Fertig, 1985.

Myerhoff, Barbara. *Number Our Days.* New York: E. P. Dutton, 1978.

Nasaw, David. *Schooled to Order: A Social History of Public Schooling in the United States.* New York: Oxford University Press, 1979.

Peiss, Kathy. *Cheap Amusements: Working Women and Leisure in Turn-of-the-Century New York.* Philadelphia: Temple University Press, 1986.

Perry, Elisabeth Israels. *Belle Moskowitz: Feminine Politics and the Exercise of Power in the Age of Alfred E. Smith.* New York: Oxford University Press, 1987.

# Bibliography

Plaskow, Judith. *Standing Again at Sinai*. San Francisco: Harper & Row, 1990.

Ransel, David, ed. *The Family in Imperial Russia: New Lines of Historical Research*. Urbana: University of Illinois Press, 1978.

Rodrigue, Aron. *French Jews, Turkish Jews: The Alliance Israélite Universelle and the Politics of Jewish Schooling in Turkey, 1860–1925*. Bloomington: Indiana University Press, 1990.

Rogow, Faith. *Gone to Another Meeting: The National Council of Jewish Women, 1893–1993*. Tuscaloosa: University of Alabama Press, 1993.

Rozenblit, Marsha. *The Jews of Vienna, 1867–1914: Assimilation and Community*. Albany: State University of New York Press, 1983.

Scott, Joan Wallach. *Gender and the Politics of History*. New York: Columbia University Press, 1988.

Shargel, Bella Round. *Practical Dreamer: Israel Friedlaender and the Shaping of American Judaism*. New York: Jewish Theological Seminary, 1985.

Smith, Bonnie. *Ladies of the Leisure Class: The Bourgeoises of Northern France in the Nineteenth Century*. Princeton: Princeton University Press, 1981.

Smith, Judith. *Family Connections: A History of Italian and Jewish Immigrant Lives in Providence, Rhode Island, 1900–1940*. Albany: State University of New York Press, 1985.

Sochen, June. *Consecrate Every Day: The Public Lives of Jewish American Women, 1880–1980*. Albany: State University of New York Press, 1981.

Stanislawski, Michael. *For Whom Do I Toil?* New York: Oxford University Press, 1988.

———. *Tsar Nicholas I and the Jews*. Philadelphia: Jewish Publication Society, 1983.

Stites, Richard. *The Women's Liberation Movement in Russia: Feminism, Nihilism, and Bolshevism, 1860–1930*. Princeton: Princeton University Press, 1978.

Tal, Uriel. *Christians and Jews in Germany: Religion, Politics, and Ideology in the Second Reich, 1870–1914*. Trans. Noah Jonathan Jacobs. Ithaca: Cornell University Press, 1975.

Tobias, Henry. *The Jewish Bund in Russia: From Its Origins to 1905*. Stanford: Stanford University Press, 1972.

# Bibliography

Umansky, Ellen M. *Lily H. Montagu and the Advancement of Liberal Judaism: From Vision to Vocation*. Lewiston, N.Y.: Edwin Mellen, 1983.

Vital, David. *The Origins of Zionism*. Oxford: Oxford University Press, 1975.

Walden, Daniel, ed. *Studies in American Jewish Literature*, vol. 3, *Jewish Women Writers and Women in Jewish Literature*. Albany: State University of New York Press, 1983.

Weinberg, Sydney Stahl. *The World of Our Mothers: The Lives of Jewish Immigrant Women*. Chapel Hill: University of North Carolina Press, 1988.

Wistrich, Robert S. *The Jews of Vienna in the Age of Franz Joseph*. Oxford: Oxford University Press, 1989.

Yans-McLaughlin, Virginia. *Family and Community: Italian Immigrants in Buffalo, 1880–1930*. Ithaca: Cornell University Press, 1977.

Zipperstein, Steven. *The Jews of Odessa*. Stanford: Stanford University Press, 1985.

## Articles

Albert, Phyllis Cohen. "Ethnicity and Solidarity in Nineteenth-Century France." In *Mystics, Philosophers, and Politicians: Essays in Jewish Intellectual History in Honor of Alexander Altmann*, ed. Jehuda Reinharz and Daniel Swetschinski, 249–74. Durham, N.C.: Duke University Press, 1982.

———. "L'intégration et la persistance de l'ethnicité chez les Juifs dans la France moderne." In *Histoire politique des Juifs de France*, ed. Pierre Birnbaum, 221–43. Paris: Presses de la Fondation Nationale des Sciences Politiques, 1990.

Berrol, Selma. "Class or Ethnicity: The Americanized German Jewish Woman and Her Middle Class Sisters in 1895." *Jewish Social Studies* 47, no. 1 (1985): 21–32.

Biale, David. "Childhood, Marriage, and the Family in the Eastern European Jewish Enlightenment." In *The Jewish Family: Myths and Reality*, ed. Steven M. Cohen and Paula E. Hyman, 45–61. New York: Holmes & Meier, 1986.

Bienstock, Beverly Gray. "The Changing Image of the American Jewish Mother." In *Changing Images of the Family*, ed. Virginia Tufte and Barbara Myerhoff, 173–91. New Haven: Yale University Press, 1979.

Bodek, Evelyn. " 'Making Do': Jewish Women and Philanthropy." In *Jewish Life in Philadelphia*, ed. Murray Friedman, 143–62. Philadelphia: ISHI Publications, 1983.

Braude, Ann D. "The Jewish Woman's Encounter with American Culture." In *Women and Religion in America*, vol. 1, *The Nineteenth Century*, ed. Rosemary Radford Ruether and Rosemary Skinner Keller, 150–92. San Francisco: Harper & Row, 1981.

———. "Jewish Women in the Twentieth Century: Building a Life in America." In *Women and Religion in America*, vol. 3, 1900–1968, ed. Rosemary Radford Ruether and Rosemary Skinner Keller, 131–74. San Francisco: Harper & Row, 1986.

Burman, Rickie. " 'She Looketh Well to the Ways of Her Household': The Changing Role of Jewish Women in Religious Life, c. 1880–1930." In *Religion in the Lives of English Women, 1760–1930*, ed. Gail Malmgreen, 234–59. London: Croom Helm, 1986.

Cohen, Gary. "Jews in German Society: Prague, 1860–1914." In *Jews and Germans from 1860 to 1933: The Problematic Symbiosis*, ed. David Bronsen, 306–37. Heidelberg: Carl Winter Universitätsverlag, 1979.

Davis-Kram, Harriet. "The Story of the Sisters of the Bund." *Contemporary Jewry* 5, no. 2 (1980): 27–43.

Dinnerstein, Leonard. "Education and the Advancement of American Jews." In *American Education and the European Immigrant*, ed. Bernard Weiss, 44–60. Urbana: University of Illinois Press, 1981.

Etkes, Immanuel. "Marriage and Torah Study among the Lomdim in Lithuania in the Nineteenth Century." In *The Jewish Family: Metaphor and Memory*, ed. David Kraemer, 153–78. New York: Oxford University Press, 1989.

Goldman, Karla. "The Ambivalence of Reform Judaism: Kaufmann Kohler and the Ideal Jewish Woman." *American Jewish History* 79, no. 4 (1990): 477–99.

Green, Nancy. "L'émigration comme émancipation: Les femmes juives d'Europe de l'Est à Paris, 1881–1914." *Pluriel* 27 (1981).

# Bibliography

———. "The Making of the Modern Jewish Woman." In *A History of Women in the West*, vol. 4, *Emerging Feminism from Revolution to World War*, ed. Geneviève Fraisse and Michelle Perrot, 213–27. Cambridge: Harvard University Press, 1993.

Hyman, Paula E. "Culture and Gender: Women in the Immigrant Jewish Community." In *The Legacy of Jewish Migration: 1881 and Its Impact*, ed. David Berger, 157–68. Social Science Monographs. New York: Brooklyn College Press, 1983.

———. "Feminist Studies and Modern Jewish History." In *Feminist Perspectives on Jewish Studies*, ed. Lynn Davidman and Shelly Tenenbaum. New Haven: Yale University Press, in press.

———. "Gender and Jewish History." *Tikkun*, Jan.–Feb. 1988, pp. 35–38.

———. "Immigrant Women and Consumer Protest: The New York Kosher Meat Boycott of 1902." *American Jewish History* 70, no. 1 (1980): 91–105.

Inglehart, Babbette. "Daughters of Loneliness: Anzia Yezierska and the Immigrant Woman Writers." *Studies in American Jewish Literature* 1, no. 2 (1975): 1–10.

Joselit, Jenna Weissman. " 'A Set Table': Jewish Domestic Culture in the New World, 1880–1950." In *Getting Comfortable in New York: The American Jewish Home, 1880–1950*, ed. Susan L. Braunstein and Jenna Weissman Joselit, 19–73. New York: Jewish Museum, 1990.

———. "The Special Sphere of the Middle-Class American Jewish Woman: The Synagogue Sisterhood, 1890–1940." In *The American Synagogue: A Sanctuary Transformed*, ed. Jack Wertheimer, 206–30. Cambridge: Cambridge University Press, 1987.

Kahan, Arcadius. "Economic Opportunities and Some Pilgrims' Progress: Jewish Immigrants from Eastern Europe in the U.S., 1890–1914." In *Essays in Jewish Social and Economic History*, ed. Roger Weiss, 101–17. Chicago: University of Chicago Press, 1986.

———. "The Impact of Industrialization in Tsarist Russia on the Socioeconomic Conditions of the Jewish Population." In *Essays in Jewish Social and Economic History*, ed. Roger Weiss, 1–69. Chicago: University of Chicago Press, 1986.

# Bibliography

Kaplan, Marion. "Priestess and Hausfrau: Women and Tradition in the German-Jewish Family." In *The Jewish Family*, ed. Steven M. Cohen and Paula E. Hyman, 62–81. New York: Holmes & Meier, 1986.

———. "Tradition and Transition: The Acculturation, Assimilation and Integration of Jews in Imperial Germany—A Gender Analysis." *Leo Baeck Institute Yearbook* 27 (1982): 3–35.

Kessler-Harris. "Organizing the Unorganizable: Three Jewish Women and Their Union." In *Class, Sex, and the Woman Worker*, ed. Milton Cantor and Bruce Laurie, 144–65. Westport: Greenwood Press, 1977. Reprinted from *Labor History* 17 (Winter 1976).

Krause, Corinne Azen. "Urbanization without Breakdown: Italian, Jewish, and Slavic Immigrant Women in Pittsburgh." *Journal of Urban History* 4, no. 3 (1978): 291–306.

Kuznets, Simon. "Immigration of Russian Jews to the United States: Background and Structure." *Perspectives in American History* 9 (1975): 35–124.

Lederhendler, Eli. "Guides for the Perplexed: Sex, Manners, and Mores for the Yiddish Reader in America." *Modern Judaism* 11, no. 3 (Oct. 1991): 321–41.

Lerner, Elinor. "Jewish Involvement in the New York City Woman Suffrage Movement." *American Jewish History* 70, no. 4 (1981): 442–61.

Lewin, Kurt. "Self-Hatred among Jews." In *Resolving Social Conflicts*, ed. Gertrud Weiss Lewin, 186–200. New York: Harper & Brothers, 1948.

Lewis, Jane. "Women, Lost and Found: The Impact of Feminism on History." In *Men's Studies Modified: The Impact of Feminism on the Academic Disciplines*, ed. Dale Spender, 55–71. Oxford and New York: Pergamon Press, 1981.

Magnus, Shulamit. " 'Out of the Ghetto': Integrating the Study of Jewish Women into the Study of 'the Jews.' " *Judaism* 39, no. 1 (1990): 28–36.

———. "Pauline Wengeroff and the Voice of Jewish Modernity." In *Gender and Judaism*, ed. Tamar Rudavsky. New York: New York University Press, forthcoming.

Moore, Deborah Dash. "Trude Weiss-Rosmarin and *The Jewish Spectator*." *Jewish Spectator*, spring 1993, pp. 8–15.

# Bibliography

Mosse, George. "Max Nordau, Liberalism and the New Jew." *Journal of Contemporary History* 27, no. 4 (Oct. 1992): 565–81.

Nadell, Pamela. "The Beginnings of the Religious Emancipation of American Jewish Women." Paper delivered at the Berkshire Conference of Women Historians, New Brunswick, N.J., 8 June 1990.

Panitz, Esther. "In Defense of the Jewish Immigrant, 1891–1924." In *The Jewish Experience in America: Selected Studies from the Publications of the American Jewish Historical Society*, ed. Abraham Karp, 5:23–63. Waltham: American Jewish Historical Society, 1969.

———. "The Polarity of American Jewish Attitudes towards Immigration (1870–1891)." In *The Jewish Experience in America: Selected Studies from the Publications of the American Jewish Historical Society*, ed. Abraham Karp, 4:31–62. Waltham: American Jewish Historical Society, 1969.

Pois, Robert A. "Walther Rathenau's Jewish Quandary." *Leo Baeck Institute Yearbook* 13 (1968): 120–31.

Prager, Moshe. "Sarah Schenirer." In *Sefer Krako: ʿIr vʾem beyisraʾel*, ed. Aryeh Bauminger, Meir Bosak, and Natan Gelber, 369–76. Jerusalem: Mosad Harav Kuk, 1959.

Pratt, Norma Fain. "Transitions in Judaism: The Jewish American Woman through the 1930s." *American Quarterly* 30, no. 5 (1978): 681–702.

Prell, Riv-Ellen. "Rage and Representation: Jewish Gender Stereotypes in American Culture." In *Uncertain Terms: Negotiating Gender in American Culture*, ed. Faye Ginsburg and Anna Lowenhaupt Tsing, 248–66. Boston: Beacon Press, 1990.

Roskies, David. "Yiddish Popular Literature and the Female Reader." *Journal of Popular Culture* 10, no. 4 (1977): 852–58.

Schorsch, Ismar. "From Wolfenbüttel to Wissenschaft: The Divergent Paths of Isaak Markus Jost and Leopold Zunz." *Leo Baeck Institute Yearbook* 22 (1977): 109–28.

Seller, Maxine S. "Defining Socialist Womanhood: The Women's Page of the *Jewish Daily Forward* in 1919." *American Jewish History* 76, no. 4 (1987): 416–38.

Singerman, Robert. "The Jew as Racial Alien: The Genetic Component of American Anti-Semitism." In *Anti-Semitism in American History*, ed. David A. Gerber, 103–28. Urbana and Chicago: University of Illinois Press, 1986.

Sinkoff, Nancy B. "Educating for 'Proper' Jewish Womanhood: A Case Study in Domesticity and Vocational Training, 1897–1926." *American Jewish History* 77, no. 4 (June 1988): 572–99.

Stampfer, Shaul. "Gender Differentiation and Education of the Jewish Woman in Nineteenth-Century Eastern Europe." *Polin* 7 (1992): 63–87.

Szajkowski, Zosa. "The Attitude of American Jews to East European Jewish Immigrants." *Publications of the American Jewish Historical Society* 40 (1950–51): 221–80.

Toury, Jacob. "Der Eintritt der Juden ins deutsche Bürgertum." In *Das Judentum in der deutschen Umwelt, 1800–1850*, ed. Hans Liebeschütz and Arnold Paucker, 139–242. Tübingen: Mohr, 1977.

Umansky, Ellen. "Piety, Persuasion and Friendship: Jewish Female Leadership in Modern Times." In *Embodied Love: Sensuality and Relationship as Feminist Values*, ed. Paula M. Cooey, Sharon A. Farmer, and Mary Ellen Ross, 189ff. New York: Harper & Row, 1987.

Volkov, Shulamit. "Antisemitism as a Cultural Code—Reflections on the History and Historiography of Antisemitism in Imperial Germany." *Leo Baeck Institute Yearbook* 23 (1978): 25–46.

Weissler, Chava. "For Women and for Men Who Are Like Women: The Construction of Gender in Yiddish Devotional Literature." *Journal of Feminist Studies in Religion* 5, no. 2 (1989): 7–24.

———. "Traditional Piety of Ashkenazic Women." In *Jewish Spirituality*, ed. Arthur Green, 2:245–75. New York: Crossroad, 1987.

Weissman, Deborah. "Bais Yaakov: A Historical Model for Jewish Feminists." In *The Jewish Woman*, ed. Elizabeth Koltun, 139–48. New York: Schocken, 1976.

———. "Education of Jewish Women." *Encyclopedia Judaica Yearbook*, 1986–87, p. 33.

Welter, Barbara. "The Cult of True Womanhood." *American Quarterly* 18 (1966): 151–74.

———. "The Feminization of American Religion: 1800–1860." In *Clio's Consciousness Raised*, ed. Mary Hartman and Lois Banner, 137–55. New York: Harper, 1973.

Wenger, Beth. " 'Girls Need to Dance': Virtue and Vice in the Jewish Quarter." Yale University, unpublished paper.

———. "Jewish Women and Voluntarism: Beyond the Myth of Enablers." *American Jewish History* 79, no. 1 (1989): 16–36.

———. "Jewish Women of the Club: The Changing Public Role of Atlanta's Jewish Women." *American Jewish History* 76, no. 3 (1987): 311–33.

———. "The Southern Lady and the Jewish Woman: The Early Organizational Life of Atlanta's Jewish Women." Senior honors thesis, Wesleyan University, 1985.

# Index

Acculturation, 8, 13–14, 15, 16, 17, 91, 153
Advice literature, 114–16, 119–20
Agudas Yisroel, 59–60
Aguilar, Grace, 34–36, 121
*Agunah*, 87
Aleichem, Sholom, 53
Alsace, 4
America. *See* United States
*American Hebrew*, 29
Americanization: attitudes of Jewish leaders toward, 96, 156; doctrines of, 94–95; role of consumption in, 98–99; women as agents of, 97–99
*American Jewess*, 37
Antin, Mary, 93, 102, 125
Antisemitism, 134–38; and feminization of Jewish men, 137–42; impact of on assimilated Jews, 150–53, 157; and misogyny, 137, 141–42
*Archives israélites*, 27–28, 29, 45
Asch, Scholem, 126
Assimilation, Jewish, 3–4, 7, 52; and class, 18, 25–27; in eastern Europe, 14, 71–76, 92; and education, 15–16, 19; and gender, 6, 7–9, 13, 18–19, 20–25, 30, 48, 93, 133, 135, 160–61, 168; Jewish historical views of, 10–12; as project, 14, 16–17, 25, 30, 48, 49, 94, 135, 168–69; as reflected

in immigrant Jewish women's writing, 124–25; and representation of women, 12, 44–47, 48–49, 90, 92, 96–97; as sociological process, 13–14, 49, 52, 94, 168; as viewed by Gentile proponents of Jewish emancipation, 16; in United States, 93, 96
Austria, 60, 141–42
Austro-Hungarian Empire, 52
Autobiographies of Jewish women, 61–62, 64–65

Baer-Issachar, Marta, 148–49
Belzer rebbe, 59
Benderly, Samson, 132
Berkowitz, Michael, 145
Berkson, Isaac, 132
Berlin, 18, 20–21
Beys Yaakov schools, 59–60
Blaustein, David, 95
*Breadgivers*, 128
Buber, Martin, 146–47
Bund, 77, 78–79, 111

Charleston, South Carolina, 34
Chicago, 97, 101
Chofetz Chayim (Rabbi Yisroel Meir Cohen), 60
Citizenship. *See* Equality, civic
Clara de Hirsch Home for Working Girls, 108–9

# Index

Class, middle: Jews in, 17–18. *See also* Assimilation
Cohen, Mary, 40
Conversion, and gender, 19–21, 48, 73–75
Cracow, 59, 70, 73–74, 82
Czechoslovakia, 60

Dearborn, Mary, 125
Dinur, Bilhah, 66, 79
Domestic feminism, 30
Domesticity, bourgeois cult of, 25–26; in east European Jewish communities, 66–71; and impact on Western Jews, 27–29, 38–40, 44–45, 48–49. *See also* Judaism, domestic
Dreyfus Affair, 23, 139
Dreyfus family, home decor of, 23–24
Dushkin, Alexander, 95, 132
Dvorin, Sheyndl, 75

Education, Jewish: expectation of women's, 29, 36, 161; and female involvement in, 26, 31, 32, 33–34, 35–36, 37, 38, 42; within the traditional Jewish community, 47–48, 53–55; of women in eastern Europe, 50, 54–59, 64–66, 76; of women in United States, 95–96, 118–19, 132–33; women's efforts to attain, 161–63
—public secular: immigrant Jewish women's desire for and achievement of, 102–5; Jewish attitudes toward, 15–16
—secondary and university: acquisition by Jewish women of, 76–77, 112

Educational Alliance, 95, 100, 107–8
Elites, Jewish, 4, 10, 16
Emancipation, Jewish, 4, 10, 12, 14–15; responses of Jews to, 14–17, 51–52
England, 7, 22–23, 31–32, 34, 37, 41, 45, 47, 163
Enlightenment, 10, 14, 17, 137; French, 15; views of assimilation in, 16
Equality, civic, 7–8, 10, 14, 16
*Etikete,* 115
Europe, 7; central and western, 7, 8, 13, 14, 15, 17, 18, 33, 71, 131, 135, 140; eastern, 8, 71, 72, 91, 92, 93–94

Fathers, 22, 28, 47, 48
Feldman, David, 140
Feminism: impact on scholarship, 3–6. *See also* Domestic feminism
Feminist movement, Jewish: in Poland, 83–88; in the United States, 167–68
France, 7, 14, 15, 23–24, 32, 45, 47, 52
Frank, Ray, 38–40, 47
*Fraynd, Der,* 81, 89
Freud, Jacob, 140
Freud, Martha Bernays, 22
Freud, Sigmund, 22, 48, 140
Friedlaender, Israel, 132
*Froy, Di,* 85–86, 88, 90; Zionist tendency of, 86
*Froyen-shtim,* 85–86
*Froyen-velt, Di* ("The Jewish Ladies Home Journal"), 116–18, 124
*Froyen zhurnal,* 120–22

Galicia, 54

# Index

Gender: definition of, 12; roles prescribed according to, 8, 67–68, 70–71, 75
—as component of assimilation: and class, 18–19, 36; "Eastern model" of, 8, 88–90; and Jewish identity, 5, 9, 18–19, 124, 168; "Western model" of, 7–8
Gentiles: Jewish view of, 14
Germany, 7, 10, 17, 19, 21, 22, 32, 37, 45, 46, 47, 52, 139, 141–42
Gilman, Sander, 139, 141
Glaykhhayt, 112
Glenn, Susan, 68, 110, 167
Gold, Michael, 127, 129–30
Gordon, Judah Leib, 59
Gottlober, Abraham Ber, 61
Gratz, Rebecca, 31, 32

Hadassah, 163
Halakhah: and education of women in Torah, 54
Halutzim: attitudes toward women, 80
Halutzot, 7
Hasidism, 62, 63, 64
Haskalah, 51, 61, 66
Hebrew Ladies' Benevolent societies, 30, 31, 32
Hebrew Union College, 166
Heinze, Andrew, 98
Hertz, Deborah, 21
Hertz, J. S., 78
Herzl, Theodor, 142–44, 145
Hevrah kadisha, 32
Hevrot, 30
Heym un di froy, Di, 119–20
Hibbat Zion, 80
Hirsch, Emil, 29

Humash, 55, 63
Hungary, 60

Identity, Jewish, 4, 9, 124; of assimilated men, 153, 160; of assimilated women, 154; ethnicity as component of, 53; impact of antisemitism on, 135–40, 150–53; and sexual politics, 9, 134–36, 153–60; transformation of as aspect of assimilation, 52–53. See also Assimilation
Immigrants, east European Jewish, 4, 8, 9, 94; attitudes of Jewish reformers toward, 100, 106–9; and attitudes toward female suffrage, 113; leisure time activities of, 99–101
Integration, social, 13, 14, 15, 30, 51, 53, 91, 153
Intermarriage, 13; and gender, 19–21, 48, 125
International Ladies' Garment Workers' Union, 112

Jewish Chronicle (London), 27, 46, 164
Jewish Daily Forward, 102–3, 113–14
Jewish Messenger, 28–29
"Jewish question," 14
Jewish Theological Seminary, 44
Jewish Women's Association in Poland, 84–85, 88
Jewish Women's Congress (1893), 38, 40, 47
Jews: urban, 4, 17; village, 4, 17
Jews' Free School (London), 32
Jost, Isaak Markus, 10
Judaism, domestic, 6, 22–24, 26, 43–44, 157

193

# Index

# Index

Odets, Clifford, 130
Ordination of women as rabbis, 43, 166
Orthodox Judaism: and education of women in eastern Europe, 59–60

Palestine, 86, 87
Pappenheim, Bertha, 163
Paris, 18
Particularism, ethnic and cultural, 11, 15, 17
Philadelphia, 30
Philanthropy, 30, 32, 33, 38, 41
Pines, Yehiel, 55
Playground Association of America, 108
Poland, 50, 60, 71, 79, 90
Pomerantz, Sara, 148
Portnoy, Alexander, 159
Portnoy, Sophie, 133
Prell, Riv-Ellen, 158
Press, Hebrew, 81; attitudes toward Jewish women and men, 88–90
—Yiddish, 81, 112; attitudes toward gender roles, 88–90, 118; and Jewish education of women, 117; women's activism, 113–14, 121–22; and women's issues, 82–83
Proshanski, Leah, 86
Prostitution, 38, 107

Rakowski, Puah: attitude toward women's education, 57–58, 161–62; critique of Zionist attitudes toward women, 80; critique of role of women in Zionist movement, 84; education of, 55–56,

76; as feminist leader, 83–84, 86–88; loss of faith of, 62, 64
Rathenau, Walther, 150–51, 153
Recreation, women's, 99–101
Reformers, Jewish: in America, 106–9
Reform Judaism, American, 109, 166–67; and attitudes toward women, 29; women's roles in, 42–43
Religiosity of women, 165–67; and bourgeois roles, 25–26, 39, 157
Representation: of Jewish men as feminized, 134, 137–42, 151–53
—of Jewish women, 8; as expression of male anxiety about assimilation, 154–60; in Haskalah writing, 61; by immigrant Jews, 125–31; negative, by Jewish men, 134–35, 169; in West, 44–47
Revolution, French, 14
Richter, Ida, 97
Ritual, Jewish. See Judaism, domestic
Romania, 52, 60
Roszinoy, 55
Roth, Philip, 159
Rothschild, Louise, 32
Russia: Jews of, 14, 51, 53, 77–81
Russian Social Democratic Party, 77

"Salon Jewesses," 20–21
Samuel, Beatrice Franklin, 23
Samuel, Herbert, 23
Sanger, Margaret, 114
Schenirer, Sarah, 59
School of the Jewish Woman, 162–63
Schools. See Education

195

# Index

Schopenhauer, Arthur, 137
Scott, Joan Wallach, 12, 134
Secularization, 52–53, 72, 167
Seller, Maxine, 113
*Settlement Journal*, 105
Sholom Aleichem Women's Clubs, 122–24, 163
Shoymer, 91
*Siddur*, 54, 56
Simon, Carrie, 43
Social mobility, Jewish: and assimilation, 48; in the United States, 30, 156; in western and central Europe, 17–18, 20
Social welfare. *See* Philanthropy
Sokolow, Nahum, 149–50
Sommerfeld, Rose, 109
Sonneschein, Rosa, 37
Sperber, Miriam Shor, 56–57
Stampfer, Shaul, 54
Stanislawski, Michael, 73, 74–75
Stein, Rokhl, 86
Suffrage: women's in Jewish community, 84
Sunday schools, Jewish, 31, 34
Synagogue: feminization of, 24–25; sisterhood organizations of, 42–43, 44, 163; women's roles in, 38, 44

Tal, Uriel, 16
Tashrak, 115–16
*Taytsh Chumash. See Tseneurene*
Tel'shi, 59
Territorialism, 77
Texas, 46
*Tkhines*, 33, 34, 91
Tobias, Henry, 78
"True Woman," 28

*Tseneurene*, 56, 91
Tucker, Sophie, 131

Umansky, Ellen, 166
Union of Jewish Women, 41, 163–64
United States, 7, 8, 13, 14, 15, 17, 24, 30, 33, 37, 41, 45, 47, 71, 93, 94, 101, 131, 135, 140
*Unzer gezund*, 114
Uprising of the 20,000, 112–13

Varnhagen, Rahel, 21
Vienna, 18
Vilna, 50, 78

Warsaw, 63, 76, 85, 162
Weininger, Otto, 150–53
Weiss-Rosmarin, Trude, 162–63
Wengeroff, Pauline, 72
Western societies, 29–30, 33, 37, 52, 53
Women, Jewish: economic and social roles in eastern Europe, 67–69; economic and social roles in immigrant community in United States, 97–100, 109–11, 131–32; efforts to attain equality within Jewish community, 164–65; at European universities, 77; impact of wage labor upon, 110–11; political activism of, 2, 77–81, 111–14; secular education of, 105; spirituality of, 165–67. *See also* Assimilation; Gender; Judaism, domestic
Women's Institute of Jewish Studies, 44, 164

# Index